THE IND COOPE BOOK OF GOLF

THE IND COOPE
BOOK OF GOLF

Edited by

Tom Scott and Geoffrey Cousins

Published for Ind Coope Ltd. by

STANLEY PAUL

London

STANLEY PAUL & CO. LTD
178–202 Great Portland Street, London, W.1

AN IMPRINT OF THE  HUTCHINSON GROUP

London Melbourne Sydney
Auckland Bombay Toronto
Johannesburg New York

★

First published 1965

*This book has been set in Baskerville, printed in Great
Britain on Antique Wove paper by The Anchor Press,
Ltd., and bound by Wm. Brendon & Son Ltd., both
of Tiptree, Essex.*

Acknowledgements

Acknowledgement is made to the Proprietors of *Punch* for permission to reproduce the cartoons on pages 31, 61, 71, 87, 99, 109, 121. Also to *Golf Illustrated* in respect of the cartoons on pages 45, 52, 138.

Contents

Illustrations

Golfers in the Dark

By Tom Scott

GOLFERS are a pretty crazy lot of people. Some fanatics will go to any length to play the game they love.

I was reminded of them when I read of a golf tournament finishing in the dark because there were so many entrants.

Then on looking through the records I discovered there have been many instances of golfers 'being in the dark'.

Anyway, back some eighty years ago Tom Morris and Charlie Hunter, who, as local professionals, probably knew every inch of the course, played a round over Prestwick with two amateurs. The game started not long before midnight and continued in darkness till well on into the morning. Two balls only were lost during that frolic. Another nocturnal notability was one David Strath, who, in 1876, played round St. Andrews one moonlight night. His score was 95 and because of that David collected quite a bit of coin, as he had backed himself to go round in under 100 strokes.

Musselburgh links, too, has been connected with enthusiasts for whom darkness was no deterrent. Mr. J. E. Laidlay, who was later to annex the Amateur Championship on two occasions and whose short game was to become so superlatively good that medal winning just became a habit with him, went round the nine-hole circuit in the low 40's in a game that started near the witching hour. He was a schoolboy then, and it is interesting to ponder that Mr. Laidlay's skill, even on this occasion, could be traced to that overlapping grip of his which at a much later date became so closely associated with Harry Vardon. At Musselburgh's last Open Championship in 1889 many of the cards were totted up by candlelight after the players concerned had raced home in the gathering gloom. It was the extra brilliance of W. Park, junr., a 'local', that gained the prize on that occasion.

Artificial lighting on the greens made possible the finish of at least two important competitions which otherwise might have needed some time extension with its attendant complications—the P.G.A. Southern Section Tournament at Burnham Beeches in 1907 and 'The Craw's

Nest' Tournament at Carnoustie in 1932. Those two flickerings, however, fade away into comparative dimness when compared with the dazzling combinations of electric lamps, oil lamps, car headlights and rockets that made light of the darkness when in 1928 four members of the R. and A. played two holes long after the sun had gone to rest.

Hats off, however, to Mr. R. H. Locke, who at Pannal in 1937 holed out in one shot with only the moon's light to show him where the flag fluttered.

It is very fascinating to read of the many punishing times through voluntary tests some golfers have set themselves. Stories abound of hole after hole being played continuously through daylight and darkness with only short breathers between each round. Moonlight, acetylene flares, candles, lanterns, flash-lamps, headlights, rockets and street lamps have all given aid to those who scorned the easy way to golfing fame.

To most of us, of course, playing in broad daylight is difficult enough without our becoming involved in the many extra trials and difficulties that would descend on us with the darkness.

Match Play[1]

By J. H. Taylor

MATCH play provides a decided contrast to play in medal competitions for it is play in which a greater freedom and latitude may be occasionally allowed but in which, nevertheless, too many liberties must not be taken.

Match play, I may explain for the benefit of the novice—for whom, as well as the seasoned player, I am attempting to cater—consists of the act of playing a certain number of holes, 18 or 36, against a solitary opponent; that is, provided it is a single. In a foursome it is a case of partnership. But the single is a fair test of ability, and it is of this class of game I am speaking. Under the conditions governing match play a bad stroke simply means the possible loss of a hole; it is not a question affecting the aggregate number of strokes played during the course of the round.

The ordinary club match is played over a round of 18 holes, one round being generally considered sufficient to prove the superiority of any one player, although personally I am pleased to be able to record the fact that it is growing more and more the practice to extend the matches to 36 holes.

The first heats of the Amateur Championship are played over a course of 18 holes, but when the final tie comes on for decision it is lengthened out to one of 36 holes. Possibly a 36-hole round might be better in the initial heats, but there is one great difficulty that cannot be surmounted. That is the all-important question of time.

Were the opening heats to be extended to double the present distance, the time devoted to the decision of the competition would need to be extended in a corresponding degree. That, unfortunately, is quite impossible under the present regime.

It cannot be denied, however, that a far better opportunity is afforded any player in a match which extends over 36 holes, and it is only fair to the finalists in the Championship that they should be accorded this privilege. Just the slightest tinge of luck, be it good or

1. J. H. Taylor, *Taylor on Golf* (Hutchinson).

bad, is sufficient to distinctly alter the complexion of the game if it is simply to be decided in 18 holes; but in twice that number a player should be capable of asserting himself, and, with the probability that luck would level itself up during the longer time, the best man would almost certainly win.

This in itself is one of the strongest arguments I am able to adduce in favour of the longer course, an argument, too, that cannot be refuted.

As regards the question of how best to play in matches, you must in a measure suit yourself to the conditions that may prevail at the time. A steady game is what I would still recommend, for many a man has before now won a match not solely by the brilliance of his own display but by reason of the mistakes made by his opponent. This line of reasoning will always hold good; it has been proved to be the case repeatedly.

If, however, you should drop behind in the struggle for supremacy it is advisable to force the game to a certain extent. By saying this my meaning is that you may accept a few risks if you think it will benefit you to do so. 'Nothing venture, nothing have.' But then, again, you must never fall into the mistake of going at things in an absolutely break-neck style.

Trying for the impossible is suicidal, although it need not be quite forgotten that the playing of a bad stroke, or the encountering of bad luck, simply means the loss of the hole, that alone, and nothing else.

Your opponent is quite as liable to make mistakes as yourself, and if you are in the proper degree equally matched, neither should be hopelessly out of the running at any time during the game. We are informed by medical men that while life remains the light of hope is never extinguished, and it is just the same with golf. 'Nil desperandum' should be every player's motto, for a match is never lost until it is won.

The method of calculating play, as I recommended in medal competitions, is also applicable to matches, but you may also watch your opponent and see what he is doing. You may depend upon it that he is equally as much afraid of you as you are of him, and, this being the case, the necessity comes in of modelling your play accordingly. I would always advise the more favourably situated golfer to play in such a way that he makes certain of winning the hole, unless something quite unlooked for occurs.

A great failing, however, noticeable in amateur and professional circles alike, is that when a player secures a tangible lead he is apt to develop, more or less, carelessness. You must guard against this. You must watch your actions with a jealous eye, and you must never relax your efforts for a single moment during the whole of the time you may be playing. Should you feel inclined to take things easily, your opponent will not be slow in noticing it. He will naturally at once redouble his efforts, and before you have had time to recover from your surprise it is within the bounds of probability that you will find your lead wiped off—it may be for ever—as far as the particular match you are engaged in is concerned.

You must of necessity play at top pressure during the whole of the time a match is in progress, no matter whether you may be leading or being led, if you desire to do yourself anything approaching justice. This is essential, and should be followed by everyone who handles a club.

Again, don't sympathize with your opponent. He may be meeting trouble on every side, but you must steel your heart and look upon him, for the time being, as representing your most implacable enemy. You are imbued with a determination to win, and win you must. There will be ample time after the match is over to extend the hand of sympathy to your rival, but leave it until you reach the pavilion. Some men appear to possess the knack of mutely asking for commiseration. But be careful, and watch that you keep your feelings under control. The chances are that if your opponent plays upon the softer side of your character he will pluck up spirits amazingly, and if he does not actually beat you he will make a very near thing of it.

So—never relax!

Tips from the Masters[1]

SAM SNEAD—The most common fault among golfers is a bad grip. In fact, I'd say in the case of the average golfer the percentage runs about 99·9 per cent. The Vardon, or overlapping, grip is the soundest. A major check point for the grip is that when both hands are on the club, the V made by the thumb and forefinger points towards the right shoulder. The pressure point of the right hand is the thumb and first finger. The pressure point of the left hand is the last two fingers. Have the heel of the left hand well on the shaft as insurance against the tendency to work loose from the shaft when you strike the ball with the left hand.

JERRY BARBER—Virtually all of the top-notchers among the touring professionals wear a glove on their left hand. Those with dry hands find the glove gives them better adhesion to the grip of the club, cutting club slippage to a minimum. Those whose hands perspire a great deal find the glove not only absorbs a great deal of perspiration, but it also eliminates club slippage. A glove gives a great deal of protection in the prevention of blisters and callouses. A properly fitting glove enables a firmer grip on the club.

SHELLEY MAYFIELD— One of the biggest opportunities the average golfer has to improve his game is to make sure he doesn't underclub himself. If the average golfer will check back at the finish of a round, often he will find he has been short of the green on 12 to 15 holes. The reason for this is that he has taken a club with which he had to hit an absolutely perfect shot to get to the pin. Eight out of 10 times he doesn't hit the perfect shot and stops short or in a trap. Golf holes generally are laid out to penalize the player who is short more severely than if he is long.

GENE LITTLER—There is no way whatsoever that you can work on the mechanical part of your game while you are playing. That must be reserved for the practice tee. You can't clutter your mind with

1. From *Golf World* (U.S.A).

16

The giants of yesterday—Vardon, Taylor and Braid . . .

. . . and two giants of today, America's Arnold Palmer (*left*) and Britain's Neil Coles

Thirty-three years bridge the gap between these two golfing stars. The dress may be different but individual style and concentration are there in full measure with both men. *Above:* John Ball, winner of the English Amateur Championship eight times and Open Champion once, and Arnold Palmer, the world's greatest golfer

thinking of the mechanics of the swing and expect to play consistent shots.

JIMMY DEMARET—One of the important things is organizing yourself mentally to keep your nerves under control. To win you must maintain your composure under fire, and keep your nerves under control so the tempo of your swing never changes. To maintain nerve control I made up a little key to my game. I concentrate on seeing the club hit the ball. I'm a little more deliberate on the back-swing.

BOB TOSKI—It is advisable to sacrifice distance for accuracy in order to get the ball on the green or in front of the green and stay away from trouble.

Too many golfers try to knock the ball on the green from 180 to 200 yards, using a club they should not be using because they don't have a good lie.

By keeping the ball in front of the green, you cut down your margin of error. That's one of the secrets of Ben Hogan's success. He always is keeping the ball in play, playing the percentages.

Most average golfers are good chippers and putters. Consequently they have a good chance of getting down in two from the edge of the green. They're good chippers and putters because they do so much of it. Conversely, they're poor trap players.

So it behoves them to stay out of traps—a matter of accuracy again and playing the percentages.

ARNOLD PALMER—Because there were so few traps on the courses we played on the winter circuit I didn't realize how deficient I was in recovering from traps until I got into a few at Augusta.

I had the good fortune to play a practice round with Gene Sarazen. He pointed out I was trying to use my wrists predominantly on the traps shots. I was so intent on spooning the ball out I'd come through with my wrists on the shot.

Now I hit through the shot with a full swing, keeping my wrists firm. I've gained new confidence. Practice, of course, is the answer to developing both the cut shot and the trap shots.

ERNIE BOROS—Practice for the average player is probably the hardest thing to do in golf. Most people take a lesson and then practise without following the tips they have received from the professional.

You should have a definite objective when you practise. Every shot you hit should be treated individually. Balls should not be hit rapidly one after the other. Many people just stand there swinging away just for the sake of hitting balls.

B

Start with the shorter irons, 9 or 8, taking short, firm strokes, gradually lengthening your swing. After you have mastered this club, do the same with the 7, 5, etc. Finish off hitting the driver and head for the putting green. Spend half your time on putting.

Before a match or competition don't practise too long—just enough to limber up. Too long a practice before a match will tire you and take away your sharpness.

Above all, relax and enjoy it.

The Joy of Playing[1]

By Peter Alliss

PEOPLE often ask me if I get any fun out of playing golf and the answer is 'Yes'. I do get a lot of fun out of playing. Of course, winning big prizes is most important, for playing golf is my living; but if I were to think only of the money and worry about not winning when things go badly, I think I should climb up the wall.

Ever since I could hold a golf club, and that was at a very early age, I wanted to be a golfer, and that can hardly be wondered at because my father was a professional golfer before me. I used to listen with all ears when he came home from a tournament and told stories of playing with Hagen, Abe Mitchell, Sarazen and the rest. I thought then I would never be as lucky as that. But I have been, and I'm grateful for the chances that have come my way.

Playing golf for a living is not as easy as some people think. For instance, you are away from your home and family for long periods, and I don't like that nowadays. I can't get home quickly enough to Bournemouth where my reception is always the same whether I've done well or not. The family is glad to see me. Then I can relax and forget the worries of trying to win one big prize after another.

The compensations? If you play well you make money. Then you are always out in the open air and you meet some great people, not only in the ranks of the professionals but among the general public as well. True, there are those members of the public who only want to speak to you if you play well, but they aren't worth bothering about. The others, the real friends, are well worth bothering about.

Then I just like playing golf. It gives me pleasure, and just like a good workman, if I make a fine job of it I have all the more pleasure. It gives me pleasure, too, to keep on trying to improve. I watch other players and if I think their style can do something for me, then I experiment with it, adapting it to my needs.

Then there is the pleasure of hitting a really good shot, one that is perhaps better than any you have ever hit before. I'm still enough of

1. From *From off the Tee* (Foulsham).

19

a boy really to like hitting a huge drive down the middle. There is nothing quite like that for excitement in golf. And I'm not forgetting the thrill of seeing a long putt go into the hole just at the time when such a putt is very welcome.

No, it's the big drive for me. That gives me real joy, and I think it gives joy to any golfer. I think the golfing public like it too, for Harry Weetman, Dave Thomas, young Bobby Walker and, I suppose, myself also, draw a gasp or two if we really connect and send the ball 300 yards or more down the fairway.

I know that when you go on a golf tournament and see professionals frowning and keeping themselves strictly to themselves you may imagine we are a pretty grim bunch. But that's not true off the course. We have many happy evenings together swopping yarns and relating experiences.

There's no doubt about it, golf is a great life and I wouldn't change it for any other. But I warn any youngster who happens to read this —it's not an easy life!

This is My Secret

By Henry Cotton

I REVEAL to you the secret of the golf swing. It lies in the control of the tension of each finger when gripping. This is the final action taken by every great player to govern the strength and direction of the shot. It is even used to control the arc of the swing.

What I reveal is the very heart of the swing for all players from beginner to ace.

Golfers tell how they grip the club, how they swing, how they waggle it at the address and so on. But all these points depend on the tension of the individual grip of each finger.

By varying the tension the whole timing can be altered and the club-face kept more open or more closed. That is why I have always stressed that golf is 85 per cent hands and arms.

I have worked for a long time on this secret, trying it out on pupils and friends. My suggestion to lots of golfers that they adopt a double-handed grip was made with the object of altering the individual tension of the fingers. This changes the distribution of power available and in turn governs the ability to gain better control of speed and the angle of the club-face at impact.

Whatever the type of grip used the tension of the fingers is the secret. This can be varied with training, but naturally strength counts because it provides a bigger range of tension. That is why hand exercise with a squash ball, cork, short heavy club or spring grips gives more scope for experiment when practising.

On those days when I am trying to play well the first test I make on waking is to clasp my hands together just to see if my fingers seem thin and strong. If they feel good I know I can play well. If they are thick and weak I am worried.

I hinted at this secret in one of my books. I made a claim about hooking and slicing which contradicted the usual dictum. But not a single comment was made, not a rustle anywhere. So I thought then that there was no point in telling any more for a while.

Until each golfer's case is examined it is impossible to say that the third finger of the right hand, for example, is doing too much or too little gripping. But this particular finger is often ignored when talking of the grip. The thumb and index fingers are important, but the other fingers are very important.

The placing of the left thumb on the shaft affects the grip of the third finger of the right hand. So does the thickness of the grip. The position of the little finger of the right hand in an overlapping grip is important. This can change the whole swing, not only for arc but for power and timing.

I hope this disclosure will start more golfers on the road to the top. And I hope it will stop many people wasting time looking for a faulty arc, or pivot, when it is the tension of each finger that they should study.

Suddenly It Happened[1]

By James Braid

(Five times Open Champion)

WHEN I was fifteen I joined a local club, the Thistle, and was
fairly successful in winning prizes in the competitions which it
held, besides doing myself a fair amount of justice in the matches
which were played against the St. Andrews Golf Club. At sixteen I
was scratch. I won the scratch medal about that time, and also broke
the record of the course. The Earlsferry course had by then been
extended to 11 holes, and I held the record for two or three years.
Consequently I may take it that I was playing a pretty useful game!
But there were two features of it which caused me a great amount of
trouble and anxiety, and the wonder is that I did so well. In the first
place I was then, and for a long time afterwards, a very bad putter—
much worse than I am now. My putting was nothing more or less
than disgraceful, and whenever I lost a match it was nearly always due
to this shocking weakness on the greens. Also I was a very short driver.
Almost everybody in the place of any golfing importance could drive
much farther than I could, and this circumstance also caused me
constant humiliation.

I could not see my way to becoming much of a golfer while I
went on driving and putting as I was doing at that time. But in respect
to the driving something happened suddenly, and in the most in-
explicable manner, which I shall always regard as one of the most remarkable circumstances of my golfing career, if indeed it is not quite
the most remarkable. Without an alteration of my stance, or grip, or
swing, or any conscious effort of any sort on my part, I suddenly within
a week was exalted from being a short driver into a really long one.
How it came about was a mystery to everybody, including myself. All
I or anybody else knew was that, whereas one week all my opponents
were outdriving me by a good 20 yards every time, the next week I
was outdriving them by the same distance; and the best of it was that
this sudden display of form was not merely temporary, as all golfers
know such things so frequently are.

1. From *Great Golfers in the Making* (Methuen).

This Man Longhurst

By Bob Ferrier

PINNING Henry Longhurst on paper is difficult. There is so much of him. If it is true that the most any of us can hope to do in our time is to touch life 'at many points', then Henry has already had the full, rich life—and he reckons there is still a long way to go.

Henry Longhurst, golf correspondent of the *Sunday Times,* a regular contributor to *Golf Illustrated,* writer, author, journalist, broadcaster, television commentator, golfer and lover of golf, has been in all things distinguished, by which one means that Longhurst in print is easily and immediately identifiable, with a distinctive style, and Longhurst in the flesh, invariably cuddling a (large) pink gin, has been irresistible and ebullient.

To distil him into one word, he is a 'blether'—but he is a superb blether. The word in this usage means just a little more than talk for the sake of talk. It means a delight in talk, a delight in conversation, except that no man can ever hope to engage Longhurst in conversation. One engages him in monologue. But the point is that the talk is so good, so very good, that one never quite notices until an hour or two after the torrent has subsided.

I am reminded of 'Monty' having to apologize to the viewers on television for over-running his previous week's programme when he said to them: 'But I know you didn't mind, did you? It was all good stuff!' As a writer, Longhurst has simply blethered in print, yet he has found a magic formula and sustained this brilliantly in his Sunday piece, in which he occasionally mentions golf, every week since the war and for several years before it. In journalism this is a superb achievement, the equivalent of five Open Championships.

Now savouring the wisdoms and calm pleasures of middle life, Longhurst is a product of a world long gone. He grew up in the 'twenties and 'thirties, only child in a prosperous trade family in Bedford, survived prep school at Eastbourne, Charterhouse and Clare College. These were the days of the British Navy, a Viceroy in New Delhi, the House of Commons the best club in Europe and the sun

24

never setting. These things have left clear marks on the man's personality and character. Longhurst's prose retains an Edwardian discursiveness. He is conservative by inclination, Conservative in political bent—he sat in the House for Acton for a spell at the end of the war—and I believe that he has lingering regrets that the old order changeth. This is not to make Longhurst a reactionary. He is certainly not that, but he is perhaps more akin in spirit to the old Empire builders, the men of Hudson's Bay and the East India Company and drilling for oil in Persia, than he might be for the good works of any UNESCO committee.

And like so many men who have taken full value from the best of undergraduate life—the liberalism, the sherry parties, the talk on every conceivable subject into the wee sma' hours, even attendance at an occasional lecture—he is a man of definite and positive views on anything you throw at him.

Characteristically, when he lived in London he lived in Chelsea. His prep-school days at Eastbourne and the long walks then over the South Downs have given him a love of this part of England which lingers still. He now lives on top of the Downs, on the ridge behind Brighton, in Clayton Windmills ('Jack and Jill'). There we talked, in the home that is a jumble of house and windmills, crammed with books and papers and paintings, cherished in a singularly English way.

There he thundered about the desecration of the Downs. 'Taken a thousand years to make them—one man with a tractor could plough them up in a week. And they are doing it.' Longhurst in his way is a civilized crusader, a crusader with a quiet voice. He has maintained a brisk correspondence in his local paper with British Railways on the subject of Pullman cars on the local line; with Sussex County Council on preserving his windmills as some form of public trust; his golfing obsessions—slow play, the pruning of a swollen rule book, and most of all the modern clubs, and golf balls which fly for miles and render obsolescent the structure and intent of almost every existing golf course—are too well known to require labouring here.

An early life near the course at Bedford started him playing. He became captain of a Cambridge team which impulsively decided to 'tour' the U.S. in 1930, scraped up the necessary £150 each and did just that, playing 20 matches in a few weeks. An account of this tour for *Golf Illustrated*, fee two guineas, may be said to have started him on a career of writing golf.

At all events, when he came down from Cambridge he answered an ad. in the personal column of *The Times* and before he knew it was golf correspondent of the *Evening Standard,* the *Sunday Times* and one of the glossy weeklies—all at one and the same time!

'There didn't seem to be any clash of interests,' he says, 'and I had more than a thousand a year. Imagine, in the 1930s, a young bachelor, all that money, flat in town, little car. What more could a man hope for?'

I wanted to know how a man of Longhurst's background and talents and intellect, and indeed life's experience, could devote a life to golf which is, after all, in its truest sense a mere pastime.

'It is less simple than that,' he said. 'The point is that golf is a game which people *play*. Unlike cricket and soccer and almost all the rest of them one plays golf until one dies. There is the endless interest. And there is the civilized background of the club, the bar, the members and the conversation about everything.

'It has a place in all business and professional activity throughout life, it attracts all society and not specific levels of society. If there is one thing I am sure of in looking back, it is that I am a classless person —I can meet and speak to anyone, and feel at home in their company.'

In this sense the young Longhurst was perhaps quick to realize that golf was more than a pastime or a recreation. For him at all events it held the magic passport to a wider world. He has gone three times round the world. He has made some 30 trips to the United States, averaging certainly one trip to America every year. Mexico City, Tokyo, Hong Kong, Melbourne, Abadan have been as commonplace to Longhurst as the domestic St. Andrews-Lytham-Sandwich circuit to others. But he will patronize no one on *that* score because he says that as far as golf is concerned these islands of ours comprise a 'golden treasury of golf—Killarney, Portrush, Turnberry, Sandwich, Sunningdale; links, downland, parkland, clay, gravel, sand, every conceivable type of course is within a 100-mile journey of every golfer in these islands'.

St. Andrews remains inviolate, a thing apart, a shrine for him here at home. If he won a million and retired tomorrow it would be to Ceylon ('Climate, dear boy, wonderful'). There are aspects of American golf which he dislikes intensely. Four hours for a round of golf ('After three hours one just feels drugged'), caddie cars ('Grown men in perambulators with cabin trunks full of golf clubs'), and, in every sense, the mechanization of a game which to him should remain personalized, spontaneous, earthy, full of rich characters *none* of whom wear white caps, *none* of whom tuck their trousers inside their socks.

Always, too, with the travelling Longhurst, 'His Lordship' has paid. Always there has been one of the great press lords for whom he has worked to pick up the tab for expenses, and Longhurst confesses this unblushingly. 'How else can a man do it, how can he spend his own money on these things after paying tax? Impossible, quite impossible.'

Another of his obsessions, I should relate, is income tax.

He has written the history of British petroleum, puttered across the Rockies in a helicopter, plunged in full diving gear into the Persian Gulf, trail-blazed for General Critchley—a firm friend of 30 years' standing—in opening new airlines to the Far East and West Africa after the war. And succeeded too.

Thus Henry Longhurst, Sussex squire-of-a-kind, scribbler-extraordinary, *bon viveur* and monumental blether. If golf has been good to him he has been very good to golf. The final compliment on either side may well be that only golf could have produced a man like Longhurst, and only Longhurst, in a unique succession to Darwin, could have made it something larger than a sport or pastime, something as large as life itself.

Temperament[1]

By John Stobbs

THIS, you thought, was going to be your day. It started badly. After two holes you already have the beginning of a millstone round your neck. You begin to *expect* trouble, and find it. You begin to anticipate missing every possible putt—and miss them. It really is quite amazing how a succession of holes can then be played without a single really bad shot, and strokes be lost at each and every one of them!

The same thing goes even more so in match-play. You are three up, or even four up, and then your opponent begins to play brilliantly, or brings off a couple of palpable flukes; and before you know where you are you are brought back to square. Life becomes once more a difficult struggle; and you feel things are flowing unfairly against you. You anticipate more trouble. It comes.

The antidote to both of these is just character, or resolution. It is in the nature of golf that rubs of the green daunt the player in his happiest as well as his most wretched moments. But a player discouraged is almost always a player lost. As with rage, the art of golf in this department is to accept things as they come, and play on regardless. Relax. It's a good game still.

It's difficult. But it can be done, as any good player will tell you.

The psychology is different in medal-play from match-play. In medal-play there is nothing in the world going to affect how you come out in the end except yourself. Aim at the best score which still remains reasonably possible to you, and play out for it determinedly. *Expect* the luck of things to balance out: if they went wrong to begin with, well then they can come right to end with.

1. From *Tackle Golf This Way* (Stanley Paul).

The Bad Luck of the Irish

By Tony Strange

IN DAYS gone by the Open Championship was played over courses which were on a strict rota and, come what may, each had its turn to stage this major sporting event. Such modern considerations as potential spectator support and facilities were hardly given second thoughts.

It was in this era of *laissez-faire* that the Open was played at Royal St. George's, Sandwich, in 1949. It came as rather an anti-climax to a momentous championship at Muirfield the previous year where King George VI mingled with the enthusiastic Scottish galleries and Henry Cotton proved that he was still a major golfing power with an impressive victory.

From the word go the Sandwich event was rather a flat affair. Cotton declined to defend his title, which would have brought him into direct conflict with his South African adversary, Bobby Locke, a battle royal long awaited. Consequently, the quality of the field suffered somewhat.

But, as very often happens when the outlook is bleak, the championship bubbled into life. An eagle-eyed championship official set it going when he spotted an odd-looking club in the bag of Charles Rotar, an American professional, who was a U.S. Army sergeant on leave from Frankfurt.

Rotar, who had seemingly qualified for the Open proper with a two-round aggregate of 150, was on the point of leaving the Royal St. George's club for an early night's rest when he was suddenly summoned before the championship committee. With him went that odd-looking club, an aluminium putter with a goose neck which virtually made it a centre-shafted club.

The committee gave its verdict. Rotar was out of the championship, disqualified for using an illegal club. The American was bewildered and angry and, surrounded by competitors, pressmen and caddies, deliberately smashed the club.

He declared that he had used it before and with permission during the Swiss Open. Rotar pleaded ignorance of the rules.

'I had it made in America and have used it in competitions there and on the Continent,' he said.

But Rotar had no cause for complaint, for competitors were informed that if clubs did not conform to the rules as laid down by the Royal and Ancient Golf Club of St. Andrews disqualification would be applied.

At that time the Rules of Golf differed considerably where the British and U.S. administrations were concerned, and it may well be that this incident, which received its full quota of publicity, did much towards the standardization of the rules. At least it clearly illustrated the stupidity of the position as it then existed.

Strange it was that another American, Walter Travis, was the cause of the R. and A. ban on the centre-shafted clubs after he had used a Schenectady putter to help him to win the Amateur Championship title over the same course in 1904.

Rotar's disqualification was a sensation but it was a mere draught to the excitement which blew over the championship three days later. It was a sad thing that only a scant crowd of several hundred spectators experienced it.

Without Cotton, Locke from the very start was expected to walk away with the title. He was fresh from a very successful season on the U.S. circuit during which he became rather unpopular with the locals because he persisted in taking more than his fair share from the prize kitty. It was a long while since a stranger had managed to do this.

In practice he lived up to his reputation. He proved to be an expert manipulator of a golf ball especially around the greens, and he was as hot a favourite as you are ever likely to meet.

At the other end of the table came Harry Bradshaw from Kilcroney, an ambling, lovable Irishman with a haymaker's swing, a three-finger overlapping grip to shock the purists and no more than an outsider's chance of taking the prize back across the Irish Sea.

The Irishman had not been a frequent tournament player and on his previous visit to England two months earlier had suffered disqualification in a qualifying event at Fulwell for playing his partner's ball. Indeed, this may well have had some bearing on the famous bottle incident which befell him in the second round.

Despite Locke's reputation it was Bradshaw who was the man in form. He opened the qualifying stages with a 67 and then led the field with a 36-hole aggregate of 139, a stroke ahead of the South African.

Could he maintain this pressure when the Open really got going and every shot, good or bad, was a nail in somebody's coffin?

Without anyone really taking any notice of him—there were hardly

sufficient spectators to give every competitor a gallery of a dozen souls
—Bradshaw opened up with a 68, a shot behind Jimmy Adams. At the
end of the second round he had vanished down the field with a 77 and
a halfway total of 145.

Where was Locke? He had performed no better and, in fact, shared
the same mark with the Irishman.

But Bradshaw came back into the picture with a 68 and so did
Locke—these two were inseparable. With just one round to go they
shared the lead with Max Faulkner at 213. After lunch on that sunny
Friday, Bradshaw was the first man of this trio to go out. He finished
with a final 70 which was a truly fine effort.

It might have been a shot better had a 12-foot putt maintained
its steam for just another half a turn on the last green. The few hundreds who ringed the apron gasped in dismay, for they were feeling
the tension which was rapidly building up as walkie-talkie sets brought
the news that the meticulous Locke was keeping pace.

But this tremendous competitor could not forge ahead and as his
last putt dropped home he was round in 70. The South African, with
an aggregate of 283, had tied with Bradshaw.

Bitter disappointment for both men and the ordeal of a 36-hole
play-off on the morrow. It was then that the ball-in-a-bottle episode
assumed its importance and a spot in the record book. Bradshaw's
second round had destroyed his chances of a second victory for Ireland
in three days—Fred Daly had pulled it off in 1947.

Few people can claim to have seen the golfing curiosity at the 5th hole when the Irishman found his ball off the drive nestling in the broken half of a bottle. It was then that Bradshaw must have thought of his recent disqualification for playing the wrong ball. He had no desire to infringe any more rules; he preferred to risk injury.

He had a slightly hanging lie and Bradshaw quickly decided what was to be done. He armed himself with a heavy niblick, took his stance, eyed the ball and bottle, went up on his back-swing, came down . . . and closed his eyes. So did his few spectators, who had retreated rapidly out of range.

Bradshaw hit ball and bottle fair and square. The bottle disintegrated and the ball trundled 30 yards up the fairway.

Because of this shocking piece of luck caused by a careless holiday maker, Bradshaw found himself in a play-off with the formidable Locke for golf's highest award. He never really had a chance after that.

The South African was cruel in his calculated destruction, not of Bradshaw but of those Sandwich links. In the end Locke ran away with the title by the margin of 12 strokes.

Jack Nicklaus, the powerful, hard-hitting American

Left: George Duncan, a once famous name in British golf, who won the Open in 1920
Right: Alex Herd who won the Open in 1902

Past and present stylists

John Jacobs

James Braid in his later years

The famous Ted Ray driving
at Deal in 1903

The wonderfully stylish finish of the
swing of Britain's Bernard Hunt

The Terror of Socketing[1]

By P. A. Ward-Thomas

THE transition from ecstasy to despair can be cruelly sharp and unexpected in most games. The bloom of a great innings may be destroyed by a second's lapse of concentration on the part of a batsman; the rugby player may have the line and victory at his mercy and then drop a simple pass; a jockey, with the Grand National and a lifetime's ambition only a few yards away, knew the agony of frustration as Devon Loch sank beneath him. The hunter and the fisherman, too, know the swiftness with which triumph can turn to failure, but of all sports the most provocative must be golf, because the responsibility is the player's alone. No bowler is there to confound him, no opponent is striving to tackle, no horse can fail him and no temperamental fox or fish can tease him. The golfer is alone, his medium is inanimate and the measure of his success or failure is the exact measure of his own ability. There is no one to blame but himself, though heaven knows golfers are as ingenious as anyone else in their endeavours to prove to the contrary.

One of the most insidious refinements, and certainly the most humiliating of the various tortures from which golfers suffer, is the disease known as socketing. No other stroke can undermine the confidence and reduce a good round to ashes so swiftly. No other stroke is so universally feared. It chooses its victims with rare impartiality, for the socket is by no means a rabbit's stroke. In fact, it usually attacks those with some technical ability, and the man who approaches with a horrid little scoop, or half-top, little realizes how grateful the socketer often would be for one of those in exchange.

It is ridiculous that a man can drive long and straight, hit his woods and irons quite confidently through the green, and then be reduced to a tremulous wreck when faced with a straight-forward little pitch. It is usually the easy shots which produce the socket because the player, in his anxiety to steer the stroke, probably fails to take the club back far enough or to hit through the ball. The result is an

1. From *From off the Tee* (Foulsham).

C

exaggerated roll of the wrists which shuts the face of the club completely and pulls the right arm away from the body and the clubhead
outside the line of flight. Other symptoms are the weight falling forward on the down-swing or excessive forward pressure on the shaft of
the club, which brings the hands too far in front of the ball.

Golf is full of tips and hints to prevent this, check that or cure the
other, and the socketer will find no shortage of advice. Usually they
act because the player believes that they will, but almost invariably the
effect is only temporary. As soon as the process becomes automatic
then other influences are free to begin their destructive work. Thus it
is with socketing. The familiar remedies—stand closer to the ball, sit
down on the shot, grip the club loosely, hit with the right hand and all
the rest—often bring immediate relief and may even effect quite a
lasting cure. But the chronic victim of socketing can never be quite
certain. There is no ready cure for the fear and over-anxiety which are
the basic causes of his complaint. A man cannot suddenly be unafraid
and confident when his senses are trembling with apprehension. Perhaps caddies trained in hypnotism might help, but to be put under
and brought round every time a promising socketing situation arose
would be somewhat wearing to oneself and one's companions.

I write from an unbelievable experience of these things, for down
the years there has been much furtive removal of tell-tale white marks,
not only from my short irons, but, shamefully, from medium and long
as well. I recall a time in the West Country several autumns ago. For
some weeks the little shots had flown reasonably straight, and then from
nowhere the socket struck. It always seems to creep up on one at the
most unlikely and unwanted moments. A golden morning at Saunton
was almost ruined; the matchless setting of St. Enodoc lost its charm
in a fury of socketing and by Westward Ho! hope had almost gone.
But in the depths of despair there came a gleam of light. Had not
the greatest of all once been a victim?

Within the hour J. H. Taylor had confirmed what had seemed an
almost blasphemous thought, and even now I can hear him saying,
'Hand me that mashie-iron'; as I did so he said, 'I was considered the
master of that club, and yet for some time I socketed with it.' Humbly
I asked how this could be and how could I be cured? 'Get your weight
back on your heels,' cried the old man, almost pushing me over in his
emphasis. 'Sit down on the shot, keep the right elbow into the side, hit
through the ball, and you will never socket.' Hope and confidence
flooded back and soon I hastened gratefully away to spread the tidings.
The next morning the sun, the sky, the larks and the sweet loneliness
of the links had registered their meaning. Never again, I thought, as
shot after shot left the approximate centre of the club, the socket is

behind me for ever. The appalling optimism of this thought was not brought home for some time. Whilst confidence lasted one was safe, and then inevitably came the day when the ball lay a little tight and one was standing slightly above it. The unspeakable thought sprang unbidden to mind and the unspeakable stroke followed.

The awful thing about socketing is its unexpectedness. Suddenly, perhaps after months of relief, the traitorous thought, 'I might socket this one', comes to mind. Or a malicious opponent may whisper the dread word, as one distinguished lady golfer did with disastrous effect one morning at Deal. On occasions like this the mind turns prayerfully to the preventives, but as anxiety mounts, so does the body fail to respond to instructions. The weight is thrust back on the heels, the right elbow is tucked in and the club held loosely, but by now the wretched mind is astir with inhibitions. In the desire to get the shot over, one is undone and there is the ball hurtling knee high to cover-point.

The socket is especially cruel, for invariably it costs more than one stroke. Even if recovery be possible the mind by then is perfectly conditioned to socket again. From visualizing a pretty pitch nestling by the hole, with a possible putt for three, one is condemned in a trice to struggling desperately for a five or worse. And the whole performance is so ignominious.

James Braid[1]

By Bernard Darwin

THE legend has long been established that James Braid went to bed one night a short driver and woke up the next morning a long one. I am now, as the triumphant reporter so often observes, able to reveal the explanation. It has been given me by Ralph Smith, who sturdily declares that it was no mystery at all, and I am bound to say that his explanation is at any rate a very likely one. Those who cultivate the mysterious and the sublime may cling to the supernatural. Here at any rate is Ralph Smith's more prosaic one.

James, he says, always played with very upright clubs, having the ball near to him and having in consequence a markedly upright swing. The ball flew straight and high but came down to earth all too soon again. Ralph Smith was himself at this time serving his apprenticeship to George Forrester, a very well-known club-maker at Elie, and among Forrester's customers was one Mr. John Berwick, a great fancier and buyer of clubs, and a very tall man of six feet four inches or so. One day he came to the shop and said that he had a number of wooden clubs he wanted to get rid of : would Forrester send for them? Forrester accordingly did so and paid a shilling each for them. Smith instantly told James of this consignment of clubs, among which he was sure were some to suit him. James sped round to the shop as soon as he was free and found a number of drivers all with long shafts and heads much flatter in the lie than his own, so that he would have to stand farther from the ball. He picked one of them, went out to try a shot with it and behold, the ball flew away into the distance. The club was thereupon bought for eighteenpence. George Forrester made a profit of sixpence and James in a state of bliss straightway outdrove all those who but lately had had the audacity to outdrive him. This is Ralph Smith's explanation and—perhaps it is my scientific blood—I incline to prefer it to that of a miracle. It is at any rate extraordinarily interesting.

1. *James Braid* (Hodder and Stoughton).

The Golfer's Nightmare
(with apologies to W. S. Gilbert)

WHEN you're lying in bed with a terrible head after playing a round at Mid-Surrey

And you wish you had not had that 'last little spot' or that truly delectable curry,

A million sheep would not send you to sleep as you think of your dreadful display,

Of the drives that you muffed and the chips that you fluffed and the putts that you frittered away.

Then at very long last, say at three or half past, you sink in a comfortless coma,

A feverish doze—for to call it repose or sweet slumber would be a misnomer—

Instanter it seems you are haunted by dreams. In the first you have wagered your shirt on

A match between you and old Jim (twenty-two) against Alliss and Tom Haliburton.

Or the venue has changed and a game been arranged up at Hoylake or Lytham or Ganton;

You are playing with Hunt against Christmas and Lunt who are paired with O'Connor and Panton.

The crowds are immense, the excitement intense; your opponents unkindly have sunk a

Putt of twenty-five yards while it's quite on the cards you will put your own putt in the bunker;

For you're frozen and numb and discover you're dumb and completely unable to utter

When you find by mistake you've been given a rake or a shovel instead of your putter.

As you try to explain, the scene's shifting again and the whole of the bar and the course hums

With startled surprise and astonished surmise for you're down for the Worplesdon foursomes.

You have altered your sex and are playing the Becks but your face hasn't changed an iota.

You are very distressed to discover you're dressed in a Curtis Cup blazer and boater.

Then just as sheer panic assails you and manic depression attacks you and misery racks you,

> it's suddenly morning; a new day is dawning;
> it's Sunday and sunny, you're on easy money, for the
> voice on the phone is just one of your cronies,
> who wants you to play him; you know you can flay him.
> You're really in clover. The nightmare is over.
> You swear you won't do it again,
> But I'm willing to bet you will quickly forget,
> And you'll do it and rue it again.

(George Montfort)

The Putter from off the Green[1]

By Cary Middlecoff

YOUR putter is likely to be your best weapon for getting the ball close to the hole whenever you are no more than about seven or eight feet off the green, and the grass between your ball and the green proper is cut fairly close. The putter also has its uses from farther off the green, which will be discussed below.

An important thing to remember about putts from off the green is that especial care should be taken to strike the ball solidly, catching, as nearly as possible, the middle of the ball on the centre of the face of the putter. The idea is to get uniform roll through the higher grass that intervenes between you and the close-cut grass on the green. The putter has a certain amount of loft (about nine degrees), and if the ball is struck too much on its underside it will travel two or three feet in the air before settling down to roll. This will add to the difficulty of judging your distance. What you should be seeking on this shot is to roll the ball along the top of the higher grass. Had you wanted some pitch and some roll on the shot, the wiser choice of club would have been one with which you could pitch the ball on to the green proper— the chip shot.

1. *Advanced Golf* (Nicholas Kaye).

The Art of Practising[1]

By Bernard Hunt

PRACTICE makes perfect is an old and very true saying. But to get the full benefit from practice you should try to work to a method or routine. It is often a waste of effort to go out on to the fairway with a huge bag of balls, take out your driver and slog away into the far distance until you are exhausted. Many times I have heard the complaint, 'I'm worse after practice,' and that is why.

I have found through experience that the best way to improve your game, and also to get the most enjoyment from practising, is to have not more than three dozen or so balls, pick a target and then start off with the short clubs. A hill, a small tree or even a tuft of grass will do, and then try to group the balls as near as possible to this target, making sure that you're not having to hit too hard at the ball to get it there. A three-quarter swing gives greater accuracy and better feel for range or distance. As you work up through the clubs, try to visualize imaginary problems—a tree in the way so that you must hit the ball a little higher, a wind against so this one must be a little lower, and so on. Try to play each shot separately, thinking over each one, and don't just practise aimlessly. This will get you nowhere, as your interest will soon fade and very shortly after that your patience. Above all, guard against the greatest temptation which is to hit the next one a little farther than the last. This creeps in without realizing it, and then the wild shots start. This is the time to go back to the short clubs again.

I find that one of the most enjoyable and profitable parts of the game to practise is pitching. If you can, pitch on to a green and this time take only a dozen or so balls. Play from just off the green and then try to hole as many putts as possible. It's amazing how the one-chip percentage goes up, and this is the thing that counts on those Sunday-morning four-balls.

Above all, don't overdo the practice. One hour when you are fresh, with plenty of thought and concentration, is worth ten of gruelling work when you are tired.

1. From *From off the Tee* (Foulsham).

Medal Play[1]

By J. H. Taylor

SUPPOSING now that the golfer has been fairly started on his way, for I do not propose entering upon the technicalities of the pastime until a little later on, he is probably intent upon playing a good medal or match game.

But it is a very real fact that the true art underlying the merits of medal play, which I now propose to deal with, is probably the most difficult of any to be learnt. Indeed, I may say that it is somewhat of a rarity for one particular player to excel both in match and medal play.

Taking the playing of a ordinary game as a test of ability, the golfer is simply set to defeat just his solitary opponent. He knows exactly what he has to do, what he has to cope with, and at every stage of the game he is aware exactly of how his rival stands.

In medal play the case is vastly different. You are playing against the whole field, and though you may be perfectly aware of what your own score is likely to amount to, your opponents are unknown quantities.

This being the case, I have not a shadow of doubt that medal play is the highest test by which the excellence, or otherwise, of any player can be tried, no matter whether he be amateur or professional.

Every individual stroke in medal play has to be thought out on its own merits, and the pros and cons of the situation and its possibilities must be weighed in your mind.

Under these circumstances I have but one piece of advice to offer : Play a steady game.

This will pay you best in such a competition. It will serve no useful purpose for you to fall into the grievous fault of attempting to do too much. You must not go out for everything, trusting to fortune to pull you through successfully.

Certainly, if you do this, there is just a bare possibility that you may succeed in accomplishing something of an extraordinary character, but then, on the other hand, the probability is that you will fail utterly and miserably in your efforts.

1. J. H. Taylor, *Taylor on Golf* (Hutchinson).

During the progress of a match, where it is simply holes that must needs be taken into consideration, it is possible for a golfer to risk a little occasionally, but he must guard against doing this in medal play. So, although I repeat myself, my advice is still, play a steady game, and leave nothing whatever to good fortune, or luck, or whatever you may care to call it.

Much has been said and written about the length of time devoted to the progress and termination of an ordinary medal competition, but my opinion is that it would be utterly impossible to play them upon the same basis as the championships. For one thing, and this is one of the most important, it would be quite out of the power of the members to devote sufficient time to the pastime to enable them to play three or four rounds. Time alone, I think, would be found an objection impossible to remove, for the clubmen who would be in a position to devote one morning or afternoon to the contest might not, probably would not, be able to spare two whole days for the same purpose.

During the decision of the championships the case is very different. Every man present is fully aware of the fact that he is there for one purpose alone, and there is no opportunity for the exhibition of any display of haste. Another thing is that only the very best class of players is represented at the principal events of the year, and while one round might not be sufficient to settle the pretensions of one and all, the quartette of rounds played is amply sufficient to divide, I might almost say break up, the field properly.

At the championships, too, as is only fitting, a man is afforded a chance of retrieving his position, even should he be unfortunate enough to make a mediocre start. This, again, is but fair, for such a test comes but once during the course of a twelve-month.

Let me give, as an instance, the Open Championship of 1895. On that date my first round was a poor one, for I returned a total of 86 strokes. But all was not over; I still had three chances remaining by which I might recover myself, and my second round of 78, third of 80, and the fourth and final of 78 counterbalance my ill-luck experienced during the first round. Here again it is a real, a very real, question of steadiness and a capacity for controlling your nerves that is rendered a necessity for the playing of the proper game.

As regards the leading players of this kind of game, I should say that Mr. H. H. Hilton, of the amateurs, is undoubtedly the finest score player it is possible to mention. He is steadiness itself, and never takes an undue risk. This is the explanation of how Mr. Hilton maintains his position in the front rank of all those now performing with the club.

Speaking of the professionals, I hope I may not be accused of any desire to praise myself, but in looking at the rounds I have played during my participations in the Open Championships I think I may be pardoned when I term myself one of the representative score players of our profession. I am not asking for or seeking any undue credit, but I must give an example, and in what I have said, and in calling attention to figures and facts, I am simply providing an argument to lead up to an explanation of the method which I employ when I am engaged in playing a medal round.

Adjust your Game to suit your Waistline

By Geoffrey Cousins

GOLF for the middle-aged is a matter of adjustment, adjustment to cope with the various changes which occur with the passing of years. Changes in physique. Changes in mental approach. On the physical side take our waistline, for example. But perhaps there will be no takers, for together we measure rather more than 80 inches.

Once upon a time we were slim, of course, but our present girth is sufficient evidence that we know what we are talking about when we say it is impossible with a 40-inch waist to play the kind of golf we could when we took up only 32 inches of the tape-measure.

As we have had to ask our tailor, or allow him, to adjust the cut of our coats, so also we must adjust our golf. What cannot be cured must be endured, and the only way to endure middle-aged spread is to make the best of it.

Of course, there are enthusiasts who actually go on to a diet to keep their waistline from leaving the thirties and entering the forties. But it would take a man with a very strong will, certainly a stronger will than we possess, to say to the waiter: 'Porterhouse steak? Oh, no, bring me a glass of milk and a digestive biscuit.'

No doubt such things are said. But we hope they are never uttered in our hearing or within earshot of those fellow members with whom we forgather after the round.

Let us now go on to consider in detail the necessary adjustments to middle-age to which we referred at the start of the chapter.

It is clear that an expanded waistline must restrict the pivot to some extent, but this need worry nobody. In fact the pivot, as an essential part of the game, and one which no doubt caused readers a lot of trouble in their youth, can be virtually forgotten. So can the wrists to some extent, for as slenderness gives place to rotundity, so golf tends more and more to become a question of arms and the man.

But please do not become a staggerer, like old Snooks at the club, who throws out his arms like a television aerial, finishes with all the weight on his right foot and, after the ball has been sent about 100 yards down the fairway, staggers back like a circus horse taking a bow.

44

'Rubbish!—you'd have been home *earlier* than usual with a hole in one!'

The club has to be pushed up with the arms, although a certain amount of cocking and uncocking of the wrists must still take place. A restricted pivot means merely that the body does not turn to the full extent.

All golfers do not go rotund in middle-age. We must admit, with envy, that many stay slim. But even for them we advise a restricted pivot because however slim they are they cannot have the punch of youth.

Now we come to the feet, and recall some words of wisdom spoken by the great Walter Hagen in his hotel room at St. Andrews over helpings of a refreshment not calculated to keep waistlines within limits.

'Boys,' he told us, 'give me a man with big hands and big feet and no brains and I'll make a golfer out of him.'

We all know the value of big hands. Harry Vardon had big hands. So have Alfred Padgham and Henry Cotton, and, for that matter, pint-sized Dai Rees. And good solid 'plates of meat' are equally helpful. So those of us whose feet seem to get ever bigger as we tramp up and down countless fairways during a lifetime spent in chasing a golf ball, need not be ashamed of them. They may be a liability, even a menace, at the club's annual dance, but the last thing we ought to do on the golf course is to 'trip the light fantastic toe'. A solid down-to-earth style pays best, and good big feet prove just the strong sheet-anchor the middle-aged golfer requires.

Sometimes we are surprised, on looking at old photographs, to see how much footwork was indulged in by leading players of half a century or more ago. With an exaggerated bend of the left knee, they often had the left foot practically vertical at the top of the swing, like a ballet dancer in the middle of a pirouette. Even Vardon was seen to do this occasionally. But on the other hand many great players like Ted Ray, Sandy Herd and J. H. Taylor were much more steady in their footwork, and there is no doubt that a good rule for the not-so-young golfer is 'The nearer the ground the better'.

Do not imagine we are advocating a solid uncompromising stance with a determination not to move the feet in any way, and use them as if the player were encased in concrete from the waist down. That would be just as wrong as imitating a ballet dancer. But foot movements should be quiet and restrained, following the movements of the hands, hips, arms and shoulders in providing a moderate amount of flexibility and a smooth transfer of weight.

So if you have big feet, remember you have one-third of what Hagen said it takes to be a good golfer!

What Golf Terms Mean

TERMS used in describing the game of golf—especially the swing—are apt to be confusing to the beginner, and perhaps even to the more advanced player. Following is a list of terms and their meanings which may help you to understand exactly what is meant when you see them used in instructional articles. See how many you know.

SWING TERMS

ARC : The path the club-head follows on any given swing.

DELAYED HIT : The act of delaying the uncocking of the wrists, or the lash at the ball, until the last possible moment before impact.

FLAT SWING : The arc of this swing is more parallel to the ground than the arc of the upright swing. Chunky Porky Oliver has a flat swing, while tall Cary Middlecoff has an upright swing.

GETTING LEFT HIP OUT OF WAY ON DOWN-SWING : Act of pivoting hips on down-swing. If done correctly hips are beginning to face target at impact and weight has been shifted to left side.

HITTING AGAINST FIRM LEFT SIDE : At impact left side, from shoulder to foot, and including left arm, wrist and hand, should be firm.

HITTING DOWN : Swinging down on ball so that club-face strikes ball before club-head hits ground.

HITTING EARLY : Uncocking wrists too early in down-swing.

HITTING LATE : Uncocking wrists too late in down-swing.

JABBING : In putting, a punch at the ball with little or no follow-through.

ONE-PIECE SWING : Swing that is one continuous motion, one that does not have separate parts.

OVER-SWING : Bringing club back too far so that at top of back-swing club shaft dips well past horizontal.

PRONATE : To turn left hand so that palm faces down. Used in connection with movement of turning hands to right on back-swing so that club-face opens. On down-swing, opposite movement (supination) occurs.

47

ROLLING WRISTS :   Wrists turn to left shortly after impact so that back of left hand faces ground.

SWINGING THROUGH THE BALL :   Hitting the ball squarely with a full, unrestrained follow-through.

TAKING CLUB-HEAD AWAY :   Act of starting the back-swing.

THROWING THE CLUB-HEAD :   Same as hitting too early, usually caused by bringing right hand into play at the start of down-swing. Power of shot is dispersed well before impact.

WRIST COCK :   Lateral break of wrists to right. Should occur about halfway through back-swing.

SHORT TERMS

FADE : Ball moves slightly from left to right. Ben Hogan's favourite shot.

HOOK :   Ball curves from right to left. Rolls farther than fade.

PULL :   Ball hit straight, but to left.

PUSH :   Ball hit straight, but to right.

SCLAFF :   Hitting behind ball.

SCOOP :   Hitting ball on up-swing.

SHANK :   Hitting ball at juncture of club-face and shaft. Ball usually squirts to right.

SLICE :   Ball curves from left to right.

SMOTHER :   Ball hit with closed club-face, hooks sharply almost as it leaves tee.

SKY :   Ball flies almost straight up.

TOP :   Ball hit with sole of club. Ball does not get in air, usually rolls short distance.

GRIP TERMS

CRICKET GRIP :   All fingers rest on grip.

INTERLOCKING GRIP :   Little finger of right hand and index finger of left hand interlock.

OVERLAPPING GRIP :   Little finger of right hand folds over index finger of left hand. Also known as Vardon grip.

RIGHT HAND OVER SHAFT :   Hand placed so that palm faces in general downward direction. Conducive to slices.

RIGHT HAND UNDER SHAFT :   Hand placed so that palm faces in general upward direction. Conducive to hooks.

CLUB TERMS

SHAFT FLEXIBILITY :   Degree that shaft will bend during ordinary swing. Three general types are : Soft (for women and older players);

A sight to please the heart of any golfer. A view of the 4th green and 5th fairway at picturesque Sunningdale (Old Course)

There are bunkers and bunkers! Here are two of nightmarish quality. *Above:* the famous Hell bunker at St. Andrews with the 14th green in the background

Below: the Himalayas bunker at St. Enodoc, Cornwall

medium (for average players) and stiff or extra stiff (for professionals and top amateurs).

SWING-WEIGHT : Relation of weight of club-head to weight of whole club.

STANCE TERMS

CLOSED : Right foot drawn back from intended line of flight.

OPEN : Left foot drawn back from intended line of flight.

SQUARE : Both feet equidistant from intended line of flight.

CLUB-FACE TERMS

CLOSED : Toe of club-head points at 'eleven o'clock' position at address. At top of back-swing club-face points upwards.

LOFT : Number of degrees face is off perpendicular. Ranges from 4 degrees in some putters to 57 degrees for sand wedge.

OPEN : Toe towards 'one o'clock' position at address. At top of back-swing toe points towards ground.

SQUARE : Club-face perpendicular to line of flight at address. At top of back-swing toe points towards ground at 45-degree angle.

D

The Universal Game

G OLF is a game for the many. It suits all sorts and conditions of men—the strong and the weak, the halt and the maimed, the octoganarian and the boy, the rich and the poor, the clergyman and the infidel. . . . The late riser can play comfortably and be back for his rubber in the afternoon; the sanguine man can measure himself against those who will beat him; the half-crown seeker can find victims; the gambler can bet; the man of high principle, by playing for nothing, may enjoy himself and yet feel good. You can brag, and lose matches; depreciate yourself, and win them. Unlike the other Scotch game of whisky-drinking, excess in it is not injurious to the health.

Sir Walter Simpson

G OLF is the only game where the worst player gets the best of it. He obtains more out of it as regards both exercise and enjoyment, for the good player gets worried over the slightest mistake, whereas the poor player makes too many mistakes to worry over them.

David Lloyd George

Hitting with the Shoulders

By Bill Cox

'HE OPENED his shoulders on that one!' How many times have you heard this term used when a player endeavours to hit a particularly long shot? It is also used for other sports, but I have never fully understood it.

I cannot see how one can 'open one's shoulders'; are they then sometimes shut? But of one thing I am quite sure—hitting with the shoulders is one of the most common and disastrous faults in golf.

A player can have an orthodox grip, stance and position at the top of the back-swing and appear all set to hit a perfectly straight shot down the middle of the course, and then, for no apparent reason, his shoulders begin to unwind before the hands and arms pull the club into the hitting area (about halfway on the down-swing). This early unwinding of the shoulders not only puts the club on the outside groove but completely upsets the chances of timing the shot correctly and the result is a weak shot, either pulled to the left of the target or hit with cut.

Now what causes this fault? Over the years I have found that players who have weak hands and those who are afraid of using too much right hand are the ones most likely to develop it.

Another contributory cause can be a straight and stiff right leg at the top of the back-swing; this almost locks the player and the shoulders are forced to unwind too soon.

Underswinging by failing to fully pivot the shoulders on the back-swing can also cause this fault, and there are still many players who, because they are afraid of swinging flat, take the club back on the outside groove; this is bound to lead to shoulder trouble.

How can one cure this fault? The club must be taken back slightly on the inside with the shoulders pivoting fully yet with the legs relaxed and the right knee slightly bent. At the start of the down-swing *both* hands must pull the club down on the inside groove as the weight is transferred to the left foot and a conscious effort must be made to keep the shoulders 'wound up' until the hands have brought the club into

the hitting area. Only then is it safe to put your shoulders into the shot.

With some players I have had limited success by telling them to keep the left shoulder *up* during the down-swing, but if this does not produce good results after a couple of practice sessions then I advise discarding it because it can produce 'fluffing'. Plenty of practice swinging so as to get the hands in good shape is one of the best ways of defeating the 'shoulder roll'.

Something to Argue About

By Henry Longhurst

Avoiding the Fourballs

THE fourball is the accepted standard form of golf all over the world and those who do not like them may as well face the fact. There are still a few little redoubts that hold out (having written down the word 'redoubt' I had my own doubts and looked it up in the dictionary and, by jove, it is exactly right—a place 'intended to afford the garrison a last retreat'), but these are few and far between. Societies that play matches among themselves—the March Club and the Moles come to mind, but no doubt there are many others—play only foursomes, and 'foursomes in the morning, singles in the afternoon' is still the rule for most matches.

Clubs fortunate enough to have two courses generally make a practice of reserving one for fourballs and threeballs and the other for singles and foursomes, but most clubs have only one course and once you get one fourball on it, that is the pace of the course for the day.

I myself do not play fourballs if I can possibly avoid it, not in order to follow the fashion among what may be called the aristocracy of golf (though wild horses would not drag from me a definition of this term!), but because I actively dislike doing so. People who like fourballs are liable to say : 'I like to play my own ball.' So do I, and para-doxically enough, that is why I dislike fourballs. Half the time, it seems, your own ball does not count, and you are only in the way of the others if you go on playing it.

If your opponent is on in two, safe for a four, and you are just off the green, which is a most familiar golfing situation, this is where the fun really begins. Can you turn three shots into two and get a half? And when you have played a rather good chip, can he hole his putt for a three and snatch the bread out of your mouth? This *is* golf. Yet in a fourball, when it is your partner who is on in two, you are a nuisance, really, if you play your chip at all. You may mutter that you will 'just have a go in case you hole it', but you know, and the other three know, that you are only wasting everybody's time.

Similarly, if your partner happens to put one close to the hole at a short hole and you don't, you are only wasting time if you go on. More annoying is the time when you have put your own tee shot close and are standing blithely enjoying the possibilities of a two, when out of the blue your partner holes a long one by mistake and you are left with nothing to play for whatever. Could there ever be a more useless way of playing golf?

Nevertheless, I sympathize heartily with the week-end golfer who wants to play his own ball and if I went to a place of work for five days a week I should feel the same. If a club is going to have fourballs— which means, broadly speaking, one round a day, at any rate for most of the year—then I would prefer to go the whole hog, as the Americans do. 'I have come here to play 18 holes,' they say, in effect, 'and 18 holes I am going to play.' So they all take out a card and see how many they can 'shoot'. Often they do not even play two against two, but simply play round, all four together, filling in their cards and backing themselves not only against each other but against the cards of several of their friends as well. When all have finished, you almost need a computer to tell who owes how much to whom, but it is all good fun and everyone has had his full game of golf, which is what he set out to do.

I sympathize with the fourballer because there are at least two occasions per year when I will not play anything else myself. These are the spring and autumn meetings at St. Andrews when, now that the entry is so big that the medal has to be extended over two days, one may only get one round of practice on the Old Course beforehand and one wants to play every shot. Not that by the use of the word 'practice' I wish to convey that such as myself set out with any thoughts of winning the medal, but to play on the Old Course at all is such a joy that one is not prepared to share it with anyone.

Years ago I made up my mind that the best form of golf was that depised affair, the three-ball. You enjoy the company of two other people; you can get round in a reasonable time and, better still, all your shots, instead of being useless, as they so often are in a fourball, in fact count double.

Furthermore, by using the points system, you can guarantee that although you are in fact playing two matches, both will go to the last green and every single shot will count. Incidentally, people seem to get muddled up about the system of sharing six points for each hole. They say it is too complicated and they can never remember the score, so perhaps I may add that the secret is always to keep the last man at nought. In other words, if the scores stand at 0, 3, 4, and the result of the next hole is 3, 3, 0, it now becomes 3, 6, 4, which in turn becomes 0, 3, 1, and it remains manageable.

The Inspiration of Old Clubs

If you have anything of the romantic in you, it must be impossible not to be thrilled to the marrow every time you putt with a putter which saw service with Harry Vardon. So I should feel anyway, and I am pretty sure that Cotton feels the same. It represents that element of continuity that is so precious in English life and history. On the other hand, to savour its full appeal, it does seem to me that one needs to have overlapped, by however few years, the lifetime of the owner. Cotton, of course, did so with Vardon. Indeed, he studied at the feet of the master and later became as indisputably the leading figure of his generation as the great man had been before him—and largely by sticking to the same methods to which some of the modern 'Shut-face' exponents are just beginning to return today.

I do not, for instance, feel that I should get the same 'kick' out of using a putter which used to belong, say, to Old Tom Morris. Though I can almost convince myself that I knew the old gentleman personally, from seeing so many of his pictures and from gazing so often at his portrait in the Big room at St. Andrews, he did die many years before I was born and I should always feel somehow that a link in the chain was missing.

Yet perhaps I am wrong after all. It so happens that I have just finished a book about the Borneo Company, who a hundred years ago joined the first of the 'White Rajahs' in creating Sarawak. They also at the same time began trading in Siam and it was their manager who introduced Anna Leonowens to the King of Siam as a suitable governess for the children in the Palace. Nothing in the writing of their story has thrilled me so much as to have in my hands the actual letters written by the King in his own hand relating to Anna—what kind of house she was to live in; how much she was to be paid (150 rupees a month was a bit over the odds, he thought); and how she was there to teach the children English, not the Christian religion as the American missionaries tried to do.

The King's knowledge of English was limited but in its way remarkable. If some of the expressions are a little quaint, they are at the same time absolutely clear in meaning and his handwriting is beautiful. It gave me a feeling of smug superiority, as I watched the current film version of *The King and I*, to think that I had had in my possession the real letters of the real King about the real Anna. All of which is not perhaps so irrelevant as it may seem. After all, they were royal and they were ancient.

Reverting more strictly to golf, there is also a strong sentimental appeal in clubs which were never wielded by celebrated hands but form merely a part of our own undistinguished background. Nearly every golfer has a collection of them somewhere. I have a good many in the umbrella stand in the hall. Even this humble item of furniture has for me this same appeal of 'continuity,' for it is in fact one of the chimney pots from the original miller's cottage which we removed when turning two rooms into one for our bedroom. Now, in addition to umbrellas, shooting sticks, one tennis racket, one cricket bat and one .22 rifle, the miller's chimney pot contains various putters which have been pensioned off, not perhaps in disgrace but at the best in semi-honourable retirement. Just poking its head over the top of the chimney pot is the short-shafted one with the patent lump of lead on the back, which alas was with me on the day my dreams came true, when impossible shots from divot marks flew like arrows to within a few feet of the flag and a full brassie shot, almost given up for lost, was found to be sitting on the green, waiting to be holed for a three. No such series of flukes and good fortune will ever come my way again. If I had only been accompanied by a moderate 14-year-old entrant for the girls' championship to do the putting, I might have won the . . . well, never mind what might have been. I'll never win it now.

To handle some of the clubs with which deeds of great renown have been performed in the past is, or should be, a humbling business for the young golfer of today. One in particular I have in mind is one which anyone who visits the Royal Lytham and St. Annes course can handle for himself—the mashie iron which Bobby Jones used for the shot from the bunker at the 17th virtually to win the 1926 Open. It hangs in the hall and, very sensibly, as I take leave to think, they do not attach it thereto, so that anyone can take it down and waggle it.

One feels at once a sense of awe, not only at waggling a truly historic club but at the skill which was required to wield instruments of this kind by comparison with the steel-shafted matched sets of today. Jones's shot from the open bunker must have been upwards of 170 yards. How many people today could hit the ball 170 yards with that club off the fairway? I remember the same feelings on handling the driver with which he won his Grand Slam, which is now in the museum of the Royal and Ancient Club. Beside it is the driver with which Harry Vardon won the last of his championships, with a thickish grip and a tiny head.

What fun it would be if one could assemble enough sets of authentic hickory shafted clubs and set the professors playing a tournament with them. By the time they had finished the scores of 30 years ago would take on a new meaning!

Getting a Reasonable Handicap

I can say without a trace of 'holier than thou' that I have always looked on the handicap 'farmer' as one of the most contemptible figures in golf or any other game—even though I have for many years been trying to get my own put up and have only just succeeded, too little and too late. As I only play in two or three tournaments a year and never for anything more than a sovereign or so, a too low handicap has not mattered a lot to me personally, but I do feel that a keen club player who likes to play in local competitions is justified in demanding a realistic handicap which gives him a rough chance of equalling the scratch score, net, in reasonable conditions.

The fellow who has the nerve to appear at clubs other than his own and win prizes off an obviously bogus handicap really passes all understanding. I am sure that the greatest case of all, the 'Great Train Robbery of golf', so to speak, occurred three or four years ago in the United States. It has gone into the history books as the Deepdale Scandal.

This highly respectable club ran what Americans call a Calcutta and we call a selling sweep, and it was won by two entrants who played off handicaps of well into double figures. Their score was something fantastic. It then proved that not only were these not their proper handicaps but the two players were not even the same people whose names were on the draw-sheet. In the end, however, they did the game a great service as they strengthened the hand of the U.S.G.A. in their attempts to stamp out Calcuttas with too much money in the kitty.

I have long held the view, not cynically but perfectly logically, as I like to think, that all that a handicap competition proves is 'Whose handicap is most wrong?' It follows, therefore, that prizes in handicap tournaments, and particularly open tournaments, should not be financially worth winning. I believe the present limit is a value of £30. If so, I should have thought it to be on the high side.

There is the world of difference between women's handicapping methods and men's. In every club, so far as I can gather, and certainly in every area, the women have a sort of Gestapo chief in the person of the handicap manager, whose duty it is to see that they put in three signed cards a year. This system has one great merit: it seems to work.

The men's also works after a fashion, which is remarkable since there is an official method of handicapping at least as formidable as the women's, and nobody, so far as my own experience goes, pays the slightest attention to it. A great many club handicapping committees are not aware of its existence and the vast majority certainly have not read it.

The scheme is laid out in a most worthy document, which used to cost two bob—I do not know what it costs now—and the sum of it was that everyone should be handicapped off medal scores from within six feet of the back of the back tees in fair conditions of spring and autumn.

With the women such a thing would be possible, because they play frequent midweek competitions and often play the course in conditions wherein they can keep their score. With the men it is different. It would be interesting to know what percentage of readers who have followed me thus far have in the last ten years played a single round from within six feet of the back of the back tees, all holed out, in fair conditions of spring and autumn. Indeed, it would be fun to know what percentage *ever* have!

All that club committees can do is to try to ensure that their more active members' handicaps are, roughly speaking, right in relation to each other. If they were right in relation to the scratch score, some would be infuriated at the humiliation of being put up to, say, 28—which is what a 14-handicap player who scores 22 points in a Stableford competition ought to play off!—while others would cheerfully go off and win open competitions with 48 points.

Experience shows that in the average club, judging by the results of competitions, practically nobody plays to their handicap. In what may, I hope, be called the senior club, namely the Royal and Ancient, the published results of medal tournaments in spring and autumn very often show that more than half the field have not played to within 11 *strokes* of their allotted handicap. In the spring no fewer than 78 players went down in the column '84 and over'. This includes many who were in the high 90s *net* and does not include the considerable number who were unable to complete the course at all.

The field for these meetings is very large and members come from far and wide, many not having played the Old Course since the meeting of a year or two ago. Furthermore 'medal day' at St. Andrews reduces many a handicap player to a state of acute nerves. Even so, I believe that, if such a high percentage of members of any club turned out to play from the medal tees, their results would be just about the same.

How to Make Ends Meet

It must now be accepted, I think, that the secret of running a club is the same as that of running a business, namely to 'Utilize the plant'. In terms of running a club this means 'getting the members to use it'. As you cannot compel them to use it, you have to lure them in by making it so congenial that they would rather be there than elsewhere. Here at least we start with one great advantage, for the English, and probably, though I am not quite so sure, the Scots, are the most 'clubable' people in the world. Gregarious by nature, they love being with other people, and the club is the natural answer.

I leave out for the moment the question of the quality and condition of the course, except to say that experience shows that many people would rather play at a club whose course has no great natural advantages, so long as the 'club' is right, than on a fine piece of golfing country where the club is dull. To make the club congenial we have to do more than was necessary in the old days, when there was more money about and we were not facing the competitive lure of TV. There is no single answer to the problem. We have to nibble at it in all sorts of different ways. I wrote glibly that I could think of 'at least half a dozen'. Well, here they are :

1. Most clubs can already 'utilize the plant' at week-ends, though much, to which I shall refer later, could be done to intensify this. The main problem, to those clubs which cannot attract visiting societies, is the mid-week period. Here I can offer an answer. Mid-week golf for women has been sweeping the United States these last two or three years. We should encourage it here. Women's work in the home is done, or should be, by lunchtime. If they have young children about the house, we will except the holiday periods, leaving them eight months of the year when the children are at school. Experience shows that once they are introduced to golf they get 'bitten' by it at least as badly as men. There is nothing like a thriving women's section to keep the club going during the week. They can be encouraged to play bridge and hold whist drives, to play matches against other clubs, or merely to 'come up to the club for tea'. With luck their husbands will sometimes make it an excuse to come and fetch them in the evenings, with a consequent rise in the bar takings.

2. The captain. I am sorry to say it, but I cannot help feeling that the highly paid secretary is on the way out and that more and more we shall find clubs choosing their captain largely on the basis of 'How much will he be able to do for the club during his year of office?' By general zest and enthusiasm a captain can 'make' a club. He can arrange a special time of the week at which he will always be present to hold court, so to speak, and encourage members to join in at this time. In many clubs Sunday evening would be an excellent time. Those who play only in the mornings are often glad enough of an excuse to go up to the club again and have a drink with their friends. The fact that it is the captain's evening and that they 'must support the captain, you know,' is ideal.

'Bless you!'

3. 'Club evenings'. This covers a multitude of sins, especially in winter, when overheads are eating up the club's income. An 'evening' may consist of a variety of things. Some clubs have run successful brains trusts. Some are able to have dances. Some can make the club available for wedding receptions or 'twenty-firsts' parties and suchlike. Film shows are becoming more and more popular—though I trust I shall not be accused of self-advertisement in saying so. It is my own experience of putting on these shows that no club has lost money on the evening and some have made quite a nice little profit. This sort of thing, again, is the captain's job. Secretaries are only human!

4. Exhibition matches. Many clubs have never staged an exhibition match. They should try one. It need not be an elaborate affair with the expensive top-notchers. Four professionals from the country will do for a start. A great many members will never have seen professionals play and will find themselves much stimulated by it. They may at the same time bring along friends, or sons of friends, who would make admirable recruits to the game, once the introduction had been effected.

5. Television. Here is the clubhouse's greatest competitor. If you accept it that, just when you want them in the club, say on Sunday evening, most of your members are at home watching their TV, is

there not a great case for installing a big projected-TV in the club-house? I believe there is. Sunday evening is not, of course, the only time. TV is an insidious lure at any time. Now that golf is being tele-vised you may also get them there for the afternoons during the championships.

6. Here I bracket together two points which I am aware of having mentioned before, relating to the bar, which, alas, has to provide the financial lifeblood of most clubs. The essence of bar service is never to keep anybody waiting. They fancy a drink now. In one minute's time they may decide against it and call it a day. The first way to speed up the service, provided your steward is good enough, is never to have the members pay cash. In this way, human nature being what it is, they spend more and spend it more quickly. Furthermore there is scarcely any pain attached to the procedure till the single blow at the end of the day, by which time with any luck they are suitably con-ditioned to bear it.

Don't Change your Mind[1]

By Ben Hogan

WHETHER you are a low-handicap golfer or just an average player I have a suggestion that I think will help both.

My suggestion is that before each shot you be positive and don't change your mind. Think over your shot and your choice of club. Then make it.

I used to be a very positive player. I would look over a shot and once I had decided on a club nothing could change my mind. Now there are times I change my mind even on the down-swing.

Playing in the Masters on one occasion it happened to me while I was putting. I lined putts up and made up my mind just how hard to hit them, then even as I swung the putter I changed my mind, decided to hit the ball a little easier. As a result, I was short on many putts.

1. *Golf World* (U.S.A.).

Final Hints on Iron Club Play[1]
By *Abe Mitchell*

1. Hang on firmly throughout with the fore part of the grip of both hands.
2. Keep the hands down in the address.
3. Push the club under and up in the back-swing.
4. Try to keep the swing of the hands parallel to the line of flight throughout. This will enable you to hit down and so with power.
5. Don't swing the arms round your body, for the return swing will lack power.
6. Let the swing back with the left be resisted by the right hip.
7. See-saw with the shoulders as much as possible in the shorter shot, for this will help your hands to go back and return correctly.
8. Get the right shoulder as high as possible at the top of the swing as the right arm cannot hit down from a low position.
9. Don't allow a turning movement of the left shoulder until the right hip has locked and the hands begin consciously to lift.
10. Get the feeling that the club-head has not left the line of flight and that at the beginning of the back-swing it travels outside it.
11. Hit down and through the ball.
12. Keep the club-face slightly shut at impact.

1. *Essentials of Golf* (Hodder and Stoughton).

A big day in golf—and all the excitement of watching a Walker Cup match at Turnberry in 1963

Practice makes perfect and here are four British golfers hard at it
(*Above*) *Left:* Bill Cox   *Right:* Peter Allis

(*Below*) *Left:* Dai Rees concentrates on the approach shot   *Right:* Henry Cotton

A Shock for the Stranger
By Joyce Wethered

D URING the morning round in the final of the Ladies Championship in 1928, Glenna Collett, the famous American player, was
five up on Joyce Wethered, the subsequent winner.

A stranger, quite indifferent to golf, who was walking in the
streets of St. Andrews bent on seeing the Cathedral and the University,
was surprised to find himself addressed by a postman in a depressed
tone of voice, as he passed gloomily on his rounds, with the remark,
'She's five doon.' What the stranger thought of this unsolicited piece
of information I cannot imagine.

The Master Stroke

By Harry Vardon

WHICH is the master stroke in golf? I say that it is the ball struck by any club to which a big pull or slice is intentionally applied for the accomplishment of a specific purpose which could not be achieved in any other way. . . . I call it the master shot because to accomplish it with any certainty and perfection it is so difficult even to the experienced golfer; because it calls for the most absolute command over the club and every nerve and sinew of the body, and because, when properly done, it is a splendid thing to see, and for a certainly results in material gain to the man who played the stroke.

How to Improve your Golf

By Dai Rees

It's the Hands that Matter

WHAT is the most important thing in golf? Stance? Grip? Power? Through the years I've decided that golf is a two-handed game, and that it is the hands which are the essential accessories for the complete golfer. The hands are the only part of you in contact with the club. They are surely the guiding force. This business of 'feel' is a most important factor, and all who strive to improve their form should become aware of it. It is the hands which produce the power, and not the body as so many people believe. There has been a great deal of talk about late hitting as the way to better golf. Of course it is, but in simple terms late hitting is no more than the hands being in complete control of the club. Most players have some element of late hitting in their game. If they haven't their swing is not a swing at all, and it is body sway which puts the speed into the club-head. This is all wrong, the hands must do the work, for they can do it so much better. To acquire this 'feel'—the sensation of whipping the club through—get an old club and around the head wrap some lead, or the like, to make it really 'bottom heavy'. Then move into the garage and start swinging it with one hand, then the other, and finally both together. Believe me, no golfer can become really proficient if he uses a body sway to hit the ball. Let the hands do the work.

Keeping in the Groove

Man is instinctively lazy, and when the inferior weather comes along the most ardent golfers think of easing up on their game. It is quite natural, and I go a long way with the idea that life should be taken a little more comfortably when the hours of daylight start late and finish early. But the golfer who wants to slip easily and effectively back into his game when spring stirs must be willing to spend some little time keeping his swing in the groove. Of course, the ideal is to acquire an indoor net and a heavy coconut mat specially made for the job. They are so designed that they can be set up in the garden or garage and offer complete safety when catching full-blooded drives and iron shots. Not everyone can afford this elaborate piece of equipment, but I know of someone who has done the next best thing and made himself a full-size practice net. One day he spotted that his local greengrocer's onions arrived in strong string bags. He asked the greengrocer to save the empty bags and then set about sewing them tightly together. He made himself a fair-sized net which he has hung up at one end of the garage! Perhaps it's not very handsome. It's a patchwork of orange and green squares but he has his own practice net and he has appropriated the door mat from which he hits the ball! The thing to remember about net practice is that you are not doing it to see how hard you can hit. The object is to keep the swing in good shape. For this reason I think it is inadvisable to hit the ball from off the top of the matting. It is hard on the mat and it can jar the hands and arms badly. Tee the ball up, that's the best way. It makes every shot easy to play and gives you a chance to concentrate on keeping the swing moving as it should.

Chipping in the Lounge!

Golf is very much a game of touch, especially when it comes to those delicate little chips from just off the green and very often over a bunker just waiting to gobble up the half-hit, half-hearted shot. It happens so often. I've seen handicap players do it, and to be frank I have been guilty myself on a few occasions. This is a shot which needs practice. With permission from the rest of the household to use the sitting-room or lounge, find yourself a wastepaper basket or something similar and any piece of carpet, half a dozen balls, and your pitching club. But, take my advice, go into the garden to get the hang of things before starting operations among the best glass and Dresden china, for things can go wrong in this gentle and leisurely practice! Out in the open air, where no damage can be done, try your hand at flipping one of those plastic 'airflow' balls into a basket from five feet. When you've mastered this target practice use an ordinary ball. It won't be long before you are dropping the ball in the basket every time. But, please, until you have some measure of proficiency don't try it indoors, for I don't wish to be bombarded with claims for damages to furniture and china, from irate wives. Once you're confident of your skill, and this is half the battle, set the basket up in an armchair and chip away. The armchair will catch and hold any of the shots that are not on target and, to prevent balls bouncing out of the basket, line it with an old pullover to act as a buffer. Arrange things

so that you can vary your distances. It's great fun on a rainy Satur-
day and, believe me, it is first-class practice for putting an edge on
your chipping. You'll be amazed how well you will be judging
distances and you'll be able to drop the shots on the proverbial sixpence. Next time out you'll be a wizard at getting down from off the
green with a chip and a putt.

A Friend in the Bedroom

Not very many people will know it, but during the tournament season
I always carry two putters in my car. One is my favourite club—the
other I take to bed! Let me explain. That second putter goes up to
my hotel bedroom where I clear a stretch of carpet and at odd times,
early in the morning or late at night, I shape up to a few practice
putts to keep my eye in. This business of putting on the carpet with
a tumbler as the target is an old one. But like many of the old-fashioned
remedies for aches and pains I find there is a great deal of benefit to
be had from the exercise. For anyone attempting to keep his golf form
in trim I say that 'carpet putting' is a must. It keeps the action smooth
and putting over a carpet provides conditions which are very near
to the real thing. As in all golf shots it is vital to keep the head still and
well anchored when putting. The essence of golf is concentration.
Movement of the head can really send the putts off line, and I
suggest you make regular check in front of a mirror. Do it like this.
Cut off a short strip of adhesive tape and have it handy. Then in front
of the mirror take up your putting stance with a ball at your feet.
When you're comfortable look up into the mirror keeping perfectly
still and, carefully on the glass, stick the tape in the middle of the
reflection of your forehead. Then look down and make your putt.
With the stroke completed, slowly look up into the mirror. The tape
should still be in the middle of your forehead. If it isn't you are
moving your head—a bad fault, so set about curing it at once. And if
you do I can assure you that more of those important putts will drop
into the can.

You've got to Loosen Up

The human frame protests loudly when its owner disturbs the day with
anything as energetic as a golf swing. Consequently golf form can suffer
badly, and it can become exceedingly difficult to play down to handicap. I have played many rounds of golf with club players who have
neglected to loosen up with a few preliminary exercises. You know
what happens. More by luck than judgement these 'supermen' may
manage to get their first drive away, but then they find all manner of

trouble and the swing has no more rhythm than a worn-out mechanical toy. Four or five holes of this kind of thing destroys the look of any round and leaves the player wondering what the gremlins have done to his game. The answer is a simple one—the muscles, like a car engine, need a warm up. I advise everybody, man or woman, to swing two iron clubs like a pendulum, first in one hand and then in the other, for a couple of minutes before teeing off. It's a most helpful movement to bring into action all the muscles used in the game and break down the adhesions. I recommend, too, that you really polish things up with half a dozen practice shots with a No. 7 iron. After this preparation in the chill of a winter's morning I think you have a fair chance of finding your game a little quicker than your opponent, and certainly you will not lunge into your shots to bend them in all directions. And a final *don't*. Don't arrive at the clubhouse in a hurry, followed by a quick change into playing gear and a dash to the first tee. This is no way to start a round of golf. Remember the best golf is produced only when the player is fully relaxed.

Keep Those Inches off the Middle

Active golfers know only too well that their sport is not, as so many maintain, a game for the aged and infirm. It's a sport that demands a good standard of fitness at any level among the rabbits and tigers. I have always believed fervently that to succeed at the game a player must always be superbly fit. Physical wrecks don't make club and national champions. Some leading players are huge men with staggering vital statistics but never do they carry an ounce of surplus flesh— they just can't afford it. I must admit that keeping in tip-top condition throughout the year is difficult. Personally, I'm usually well overweight by the time March comes around, and I go into training with the Arsenal footballers at their London headquarters. Going through manager Billy Wright's training routines quickly burns up that extra inch or so which has crept on round the middle. Not everybody has the opportunity of using modern gymnasia equipment, but don't be lulled into doing nothing about surplus flesh. There's a great deal that you can do to keep the muscles tuned up. I'm a great believer in the old-fashioned 'press-ups'. Don't overdo it—work up to half a dozen a day and the effort will pay handsome dividends. The exercise will do you the world of good the year round. Not everybody enjoys gardening, but it can help your golf. At my own club I regularly go out on the course armed with a saw to clear away broken trees and dangerous branches. And at Christmas I saw up a good pile of logs for the Yuletide fire. This is an exercise which helps to strengthen the muscles in the back and right arm. It's a thought to remember when being

badgered by the wife to tidy up the garden. Strong arms and wrists
are essential both to the long- and short-handicap golfers.

The Deadliest Weapon

When all is said and done the one shot that counts most in golf is
the putt. No matter whether the player is a scratch man or a rabbit
he can destroy the effect of good driving and accurate iron shots if he
fails to sink his putts on the green. In these days of technical proficiency, championship titles are won and lost as a putt slips into
the hole or glides past. Through the years every conceivable method
and gimmick has been given a trial in this putting business. The Royal
and Ancient Golf Club has been disturbed from time to time by the
attempts, mainly from America, to gain an advantage with putters

with goose necks, centre shafts, prisms, and other devices. Indeed, the R. and A. banned some of these instruments until the unification of rules with the U.S. Golf Association in 1951. Nevertheless, although one or two of these clubs are now legal, the majority of players have stuck to the traditional bladed putter. I suppose more hours are devoted to finding the secret of putting than in any other aspect of the game. Putting is very much a matter of personal like and dislike, but I'm still a believer in the traditional method which I believe cuts down the errors of misjudgement. Although I use a double-handed grip, without overlapping for my shots from tee to green, it may surprise you that I use a reverse overlapping grip—the first finger of the left hand over the last two fingers of the right hand—for my putts. But this again is a personal fad and there is no reason whatsoever why you should not use your usual grip or a two-handed one. I'm a great believer in the fact that the putting stance should bring the player's head well over the ball. Now here's the vital movement. Take the club-head back square to the line of putt, don't lift the club more than in inch or two off the ground and restrict the back-swing. The advice is to restrict as far as possible all movement which can vary and bring the club-head into faulty contact with the ball. There are many other factors that affect the run of the ball—the texture of grass, dry or damp conditions, and the slope of the ground. Weighing up these aspects is the vital reading of a green, and it is experience alone which can help here. But remember one thing—never 'go chicken' on a putt. Always tell yourself that you will sink it, come what may.

'Jock's Niblick'[1]

By Surgeon-Captain Campbell Ross

Come, bairnies, put away your toys
    And gather round Nurse's knee,
And I'll tell you the tale of an old golf-club
    And a stroke that it played at sea.

Young Jock MacBeth was a likely lad,
    Abraw up-standing chiel,
Who was always game for a round of golf
    Or to dance in an eightsome reel.

At golf Jock could hit a mighty ball
    With a well-timed flick of the wrist,
But he sliced and he pulled and indeed for him
    The fairway just didn't exist.

Yet due to the number of times he found
    His ball in some dreadful spot,
There was never a golfer could vie with Jock
    In playing a niblick shot.

And many a night as he lovingly wiped
    His clubs with an oily rag,
Caressing his niblick he'd proudly say,
    'Yere the gr-randest club in ma bag.'

Now it came to pass that his firm sent Jock
    Overseas on a business trip,
And he took his clubs and his books on golf
    To study on board the ship.

1. *South African Golf.*

In the boat as well was a winsome lass,
    And right from the journey's start
Kate Kerr's fair hair and her bonny face
    Played havoc with Jock's young heart.

To the love-lorn loon young Kate appeared
    As fair as the evening star,
But Jock was a shy and a bashful man
    And he worshipped her from afar.

While Jock would solace his aching heart
    By reading great golfing tomes,
Kate played deck-quoits with FitzHoward Smith,
    A ruthless wrecker of homes.

Smith was smartly dressed, had well-groomed hair
    And his manner was suave and cool,
But under his Cambridge blazer beat
    A heart of the Borstal School.

One night Smith lured the innocent girl
    To a corner behind a boat,
To show her the Southern Cross—a ruse
    Oft used by the villain afloat.

It happened that Jock that night to ease
    His long pent-up emotion,
Had taken his favourite club to whang
    Some old balls into the ocean.

On the high boat-deck he teed a ball,
    And was waggling his niblick when
He heard a sob and muffled cry
    From the lee of boat number ten.

Jock stepped round the boat with a silent tread,
    Drawn there I am sure by fate,
And he saw this scum of the underworld
    Assaulting his lovely Kate.

FitzHoward was holding the struggling girl,
    A gleam in his wolf-like eyes,
His hand pressed over her tender mouth
    To stifle her feeble cries.

'Oh, Mhic-an-Ghalla,' said Jock MacBeth
   In the beautiful Gaelic tongue,
As up and round in a graceful arc
   The heavy club he swung.

And he hit the brute with a vicious crack,
   Like the stroke of an old-time flail,
On the spot where the 'Early Fish-hoek Man'
   Wore his prehistoric tail.

The niblick head tore a gaping rent
   In FitzHoward's best Sunday breeks,
And raised such a bruise on his you know where
   That he could not sit down for weeks.

Dumbfounded and scared, Smith dropped his prey,
   With a loud ear-splitting yell,
And raced away from the fatal spot
   As if chased by a fiend from Hell.

And he stubbed his toe on an iron cleat,
   As forrard he blindly fled,
Then tripped on the ladder and crashed, to land
   Below on the back of his head.

Meanwhile Jock raised the fainting girl,
   Soothed her and calmed her fears,
Whispered burning words of love
   As he tenderly dried her tears.

And Kate responded with parted lips
   To the kisses he rained upon her,
And she also kissed with a thankful heart
   The niblick that saved her honour.

And that, my dears, is the story true
   Of the niblick of Jock MacBeth,
That saved the girl on the high boat-deck
   From 'a fate that's worse than death'.

My Partner, Ben Hogan[1]

By Jimmy Demaret

B EN used to remind me of a mole, the common garden variety that digs deep into the ground whenever approached by man or animal. Even on the street or in a hotel lobby he didn't seem to have two words to spare for either friend or stranger. He was all business twenty-four hours a day—his mind constantly at work on the next shot, the next hole, the next tournament.

But this running stopped with the accident. For a while they thought he wouldn't live, then that he'd never walk again, finally that he'd never play another round of golf. It was a different Hogan who left the hospital that day at El Paso. He was glad simply to be alive. The changes in a man that a brush with death can bring about are pretty hard for most of us to understand. Suddenly he found that all this running was simply leaving him out of breath. He'd get back to the top of the golf heap, all right, but without running. He began to take time out for the little things. . . . Three years later, after he won the British Open, a press conference was held for him in New York which was attended by a couple of hundred news and television reporters. The room in which the interview was held was a sweating, stifling hot box. But Ben sat there, amiably, and went out of his way to answer any and all questions. As the tiring hour-long interview broke up, I heard a reporter remark: 'He's certainly a changed little guy. Why I remember how mad he got back in 1946 . . .'

Ben changed when he found out that life was pretty wonderful if you could live it without pain and fear. It altered his whole attitude towards people. He found out that people truly cared about him.

1. *My Partner, Ben Hogan* (Peter Davis).

76

International Situation

By Tony Strange

SCARBOROUGH, famed for its fiery political conferences and homely cricket festivals, had never known such hours of speculation and international intrigue. Never before had this Yorkshire holiday resort found itself the cauldron of an international situation, even though it only rocked the rather limited world of golf.

The year was 1949 and the occasion was the first post-war Ryder Cup match to be played in Britain. Full marks to Scarborough, who strove to make this clash between the professional golfers of Great Britain and the United States a majestic piece of sporting showmanship on the attractive and well-trimmed Ganton course.

The teams had played their final practice shots, and under the captaincy of a car-crash-crippled Ben Hogan the Americans had displayed some astonishing form and emerged hot favourites.

Hogan was a difficult man to know on this his first visit to Britain. He was loath to talk and when he did he wasted not a single word. He was a quiet, almost pathetic, little man, and his sudden and shock demand for an inspection of all clubs on the evening before the first day's play destroyed the placid garden-party atmosphere of the occasion.

His decision was all the more surprising, for only 24 hours previously Hogan had denied that he intended to reciprocate the action of Henry Cotton when, as British team captain in America in 1947, he disputed the legality of a number of clubs being used by the Americans. But no one was really worried and most people imagined that the American was playing a game of 'tit for tat'. But what Hogan found hobbling on those two badly crushed legs of his was the most staggering surprise in British golf history.

It was not just one British club which did not meet with his approval but an entire set of 14 and three other single clubs. Hogan wanted the rough faces of these clubs filed down, for he maintained

77

that the rough surfaces provided a player with unfair control of the ball.

That was at 5.30 p.m. and there and then a rusty niblick belonging to Sam King and a pitching iron and a No. 8 iron from the bag of Arthur Lees were filed down. The adjustments were accepted by Hogan.

But the set of clubs belonging to Dick Burton remained. It was agreed that these clubs should be taken into Scarborough to the Grand Hotel for judgement by Bernard Darwin, then chairman of the Royal and Ancient Rules of Golf Committee.

Then the fun started. The peace of the marble halls was shattered as newspapermen, players, officials and the rubbernecks crowded into the splendid lounge. Every armchair was occupied and spectators took up grandstand seats on the elegant stairway.

Tension rose. The minutes and the hours went by. Where was Mr. Darwin? Newspapers demanded stories from their reporters and the internal loudspeaker system constantly tore through the speculative chatter and rumours of Hogan's determination to call off the match.

Hours went by. Mr. Darwin had been telephoned. He was in his bath. He would inspect the clubs after dinner. The situation could only arise in Britain.

Through it all Dick Burton vigorously maintained that Hogan did not know what he was talking about, or words to that effect, and that the clubs were in order.

It was well nigh midnight when an entourage of officials, the two captains, Charles Whitcombe and Ben Hogan, and the corps of newspapermen paraded across the floor of the lounge into a private room to hear the verdict.

Mr. Darwin, a great master of words and letters, wrapped up the issue in eloquent phrases designed to ease the tension and soothe out the turbulence, and ended his summing up by saying, 'There is nothing a little filing will not put right.'

This was followed up by a joint statement from the two sides which modestly said, 'With certain modifications which will be made the clubs will be satisfactory.'

And so it seemed was the end of a rather unpleasant day and Britain and America were friends again. But not a bit of it.

The following morning, after the file had been run over all Burton's clubs before play in the foursomes began, Hogan again rejected them.

Again Burton's clubs were put into the vice and filed down, and on the third inspection Hogan nodded his head in approval and the Ryder Cup match was on.

And if there was a smear on the British team after this astonishing wrangle they quickly removed it by winning the first day's play by three matches to one. But a British victory at Ganton failed to materialize and the American team, one of the most perplexing collection of golfing individuals ever to visit this country, left for home with a 7—5 victory and the little gold Ryder Cup in their baggage.

Playing in the Moonlight[1]

By Harry Vardon

(Six times Open Champion)

I NEVER took very kindly to schooling, and was more in my element when I was playing truant, which I am now sorry to say I did very frequently. I was rather good at games, and I think that cricket attracted me most to begin with. I often used to feel that I should like to get on well at it, and play a very good game. But when I was only seven golf first came into my life, though in a very small way to begin with. Such a thing as golf had never been heard of in Jersey up to that time, but one Sunday a little group of strangers from England came on to the common land round about Grouville and began to survey it after a fashion and to mark places where, as we afterwards discovered, they intended to place their greens and tees. When the word went round that they were making preparations to play some new game called golf the people were very indignant, particularly the tenant-farmers, and there was loud talk of expelling them in some way or other. But the visitors took the precaution to make their position secure, and they went on marking out their course without any interference from anyone. They had not a difficult task, for the land was practically a golf links already made, with natural sand hazards and everything else in first-class condition. The grass was short and springy, and there was really nothing to do except put the roller on to it and the greens were ready. The course that was made was along the sea coast, and the club which had its headquarters there is now known as the Royal Jersey. At that time it rented rooms at a little inn which was rechristened the Golf Inn, and the club still makes its headquarters there, though on a rather larger scale than it did at first.

Golfers in England soon heard of this good new course that had been made in Jersey, and they came over in numbers to play the game on it, so that very soon we boys were quite familiar with golf, and the more we saw of it, the more did we think there was in it,

1. From *Great Golfers in the Making* (Methuen).

The face is familiar, the pose is not. No, it is not Henry Cotton but his brother
Leslie, who is a keen trumpeter, as well as being an expert golfer

One of the finest stylists ever known to British golf—the great Henry Cotton, three times Open Champion

The fabulous Australian star, Peter Thomson, four times winner of the Open Championship. He is pictured on the 9th tee at Southport

and the greater was our desire to play it for ourselves. Of course, we were all drafted into the service of the players as caddies, and we studied their strokes carefully until we felt that the time had come for making some effort to execute them for ourselves. But we had no clubs and no balls, nobody to give them to us and no money to buy them with. So we agreed that the only thing to do was to use large white marbles, which we called taws, for balls, and make our clubs as best we could. There were no links either, but there was plenty of spare land, and the construction of a three-hole course for ourselves was a very simple matter. We did not intend to set ourselves too stiff a task, for we were very little boys, and so we thought that holes that were fifty yards long were quite long enough.

Our first experiments at club-making were rather difficult, but we managed very well in the circumstances. We cut thick branches from a lady oak tree, and sawed off a few inches at a time from them, which pieces we shaped into the heads of our clubs. Then we chose sticks of white or black thorn for shafts, and when we had trimmed them nicely we bored holes through the heads that we had made and fastened the sticks into them. Then our drivers were complete. Later on we found that the heads, being quite unseasoned when we used them, were too much inclined to chip and crack, and that they lasted but a very short time in consequence. This was rather a serious trouble, and to get over it we decided to sheathe them in tin. When our parents were out of the way we borrowed their tools for the purpose, and by dint of practice managed to make a very good job of it, so that our drivers were converted into something in the nature of brassies.

With these clubs we managed to drive what were for us very fair balls. We used most frequently to play in the moonlight, which always seemed unusually bright at Jersey. We had no difficulty in hitting our balls in it, but there was trouble when we came to try to find them afterwards, and so we usually sent one or two of us ahead to see where they went to, and these lookers-out came back for their strokes while we went forward to see where theirs went to. The party on the second look-out frequently took advantage of the situation and the dim light to give their own balls a sly kick forwards to the hole. No doubt it was very improper to do so, but we did not trouble ourselves very much about the laws of golf, or even the most elementary considerations of what was right and wrong in games at that early period in our history. However, without any kicking, we often got threes at our 50-yard holes, and in the moonlight and with such clubs and such balls those were not very discreditable performances.

In due course of time, as we got on in the game and as there was

F

more of it at Grouville, we came into the possession of real clubs and balls. At first only broken clubs came our way, and we had to put new shafts into them in the same manner that we did in those of our own make throughout. Then some golfers who took an interest in us gave us undamaged clubs, and we progressed at a greater rate.

It All Depends

G OLF is a test of temper, a trial of honour, a revealer of character. It affords a chance to play the man and act the gentleman. It means going out into God's out-of-doors, getting close to nature, fresh air, exercise, a sweeping away of the mental cobwebs, genuine re-creation of the tired tissues. It is a cure for care—and antidote to worry. It includes companionship with friends, social intercourse, opportunities for courtesy, kindliness and generosity to an opponent. It promotes not only physical health but moral force.

David Robertson Forgan

G OLF increases the blood pressure, ruins the disposition, spoils the digestion, induces neurasthenia, hurts the eyes, callouses the hands, ties kinks in the nervous system, debauches the morals, drives men to drink or homicide, breaks up the family, turns the ductless glands into internal warts, corrodes the pneumo-gastric nerve, breaks off the edges of the vertebrae, induces spinal meningitis and progressive mendacity, and starts angina pectoris.

Dr. A. S. Lamb (McGill University)

S T. ANDREWS! they say that thy glories are gone,
    That thy streets are deserted, thy castles o'er-thrown :
If thy glories be gone, they are only, methinks,
As it were, by enchantment, transferr'd to thy Links.
Though thy streets be not now, as of yore, full of prelates,
Of abbots and monks, and hot-headed zealots,
Let none judge us rashly, or blame us as scoffers,
When we say that instead there are Links full of Golfers,

With more of good heart and good feeling among them
Than the abbots, the monks, and the zealots who sung them :
We have red coats and bonnets, we've putters and clubs;
The green has its bunkers, its hazards, and rubs;
At the long hole across we have biscuits and beer,
And the Hebes who sell it give zest to the cheer :
If this makes not up for the pomp and the splendour
Of mitres, and murders, and mass—we'll surrender;
If golfers and caddies be not better neighbours
Than abbots and soldiers with crosses and sabres,
Let such fancies remain with the fool who so thinks,
While we toast old St. Andrews, its Golfers and Links.

George Fullerton Carnegie.
From 'Golfiana' (1833).

This Wonderful Game of Golf

By Geoffrey Cousins

EVER since Mary Queen of Scots was criticized for playing golf in the fields of Seton only two days after the death of Darnley, men —and women—have talked, laughed and lost their tempers about the game. At first only in Scotland; then, after a long interval, in England; and eventually this wonderful game, with all its joys, and frustrations, its complications and compensations, was carried from these islands to the four quarters of the globe, where it is now played in practically every civilized country.

In its essentials golf has not changed with the centuries. It still requires the propulsion of a small missile to a given target by a series of strokes with a suitable implement. In the very beginning golfers were not very particular about the accessories. Anything reasonably round, even a pebble, might serve for a ball; and the propelling means would be any suitable piece of wood, culled from a hedge or salvaged from the beach, and rudely adapted to the purpose.

There is, and always will be, some doubt whether the idea of golf originated in Scotland or on the Continent. Certainly the idea of hitting something along the ground with a stick must have been as old as ancient Greece. Yet there can be little doubt that certain games played in Holland and Belgium, the former on ice and the latter across country, were variations which must have appealed to Scottish adventurers, soldiers and political refugees living in the Lowlands during troublous times. It is probable, and not to be refuted by any evidence to the contrary, that the Scottish form of golf owes its existence to some of these emigrants returning to their native land, disembarking at Edinburgh, and finding at nearby Leith suitable terrain over which to emulate the feats they had seen while abroad.

The transfer of the Dutch 'kolf' or Belguim 'chole' into our game of golf might not have been so easily accomplished had any but Scots been the agents. The improvisation which must have been necessary would commend itself to that thrifty nation. A crooked stick, a roundish missile and a stretch of public land—all that came after-wards sprang from such humble beginnings. It is impossible to com-pare the ancient past with the chromium-plated present, but golf as it was known in the narrow, strait-laced world of the Stuarts has become a world-wide pastime for millions and big business for those who have cashed in on the boom.

From Tokyo to Toledo, from Montreal to Melbourne, factories are turning out the glittering products of the modern club-making design. The world's greatest players make millionaire incomes by their prowess. The golf courses of the world are bursting at the seams with addicts seeking elbow room in which to swing a steel-shafted club at a small white ball which has the laugh on them in the end. And in the princi-pal golf-playing countries speculators are busy setting-up par-three courses, night-driving ranges and other means of feeding the golf-hungry populations.

Of course, golf was a well-known game in Scotland long before Mary took to it as a solace for the loss of her husband. Throughout the troubled times before the Union it had been bracketed with football as inimical to the defence of Scotland, in that addiction to these games affected the practice of archery and other warlike activities. But golf, like football, survived edicts and proscriptions, and possibly thrived for the very reason that it was frowned upon in high places and regarded as an un-Christian activity for the Sabbath.

Golf was never out of favour among the Scottish nobles, no matter what restrictions might be placed on the common herd, and when James VI came to London as James I he and his retinue from across the Border naturally looked for somewhere to indulge in the favourite pastime of 'The Goff'. So ere long we find James and his court re-pairing to Blackheath, on the eastern outskirts of the capital, where they found a waste of country with thick grass, pits and various other hazards which would serve as a fair substitute for the links of Leith.

The first recorded game of golf at Blackheath took place in 1608 and on this flimsy evidence was based the assertion, long since dis-counted, that the history of the Royal Blackheath Golf Club went back more than 300 years. There were, of course, no such organizations as clubs in those days, but there can be little doubt that from very early in the reign of the Stuart dynasty men of wealth and rank resorted to Blackheath for golf, and that on this stretch of bare commonland, where organized golf is no longer played, were sown the seeds of the game as a world-wide pastime.

The earliest date given for the existence of what we would recognize as a golf club is 1735 when, it is claimed, the Edinburgh Burgess Golfing Society (now the Royal Burgess) was founded. On the evidence

'I think I'm improving. I lost my first ball today.'

of surviving minute-books the Gentlemen Golfers of Edinburgh (now the Honourable Company of Edinburgh Golfers) can claim pride of place with records going back to 1744. Then came the Royal and Ancient Golf Club (as the Society of St. Andrews Golfers) in 1754. During the next 100 years 29 other golf clubs were formed, all but three in Scotland. The others, Old Manchester in 1818, Royal Calcutta in 1829 and Royal Bombay in 1842, were perhaps natural offshoots from the parent stem, since wherever Scots went in search of fortune they would take with them their beloved game, and form clubs where they congregated in sufficient numbers.

By the middle of the nineteenth century English sportsmen accustomed to go across the Border for relaxation after the London season were being introduced to golf, and to this circumstance may be attributed the formation of a club at fashionable Pau in 1857—the first on the Continent. By this date golf was being played at various places in England and in 1864 devotees who had for some years played on Northam Burrows at Westward Ho! founded the North Devon and West of England Golf Club, which now reigns supreme as the Royal North Devon Golf Club, oldest in England to be still using the original grounds.

In 1754 the Gentlemen Golfers of Edinburgh organized the first known golf competition and produced the first known set of rules. Ten years later St. Andrews followed suit and so began the long history of the ruling body of the game and the long chain of events leading unbroken to the present day. But for many years the game remained an expensive and exclusive pastime, indulged in by gentlemen of independent means and unlimited leisure, who employed caddies to carry their clubs and played matches for money or claret of whatever stake might be decided upon during their frequent meetings. The demand for implements was small, and easily satisfied by a few makers of clubs and balls who lived and worked in the recognized centres of the game—Leith, St. Andrews and Prestwick. Clubs carried the unmistakeable marks of the particular craftsmen, and were fashioned from indigent materials. Beech was most frequently used for club-heads, and these were laboriously fashioned by hand, then spliced and bound by twine to shafts made from suitable lengths of blackthorn or ash. The ball was made from segments of leather stitched together and filled with feathers. As many feathers as would go into a top hat were boiled and then forced into the remaining orifice of the bag. When full to bursting the final stitching was made and the ball hammered all round to achieve a fair degree of roundness.

Ball-making was a long and therefore costly business, and the 'featheries' were not durable, being easily affected by damp and ill-directed blows. This circumstance made golf an expensive pastime, but in the middle of the nineteenth century an accidental happening changed the whole aspect of the game and went far towards establishing it as a universal sport.

An exporter of goods from India, anxious to get protection for his wares during the long journey to Britain, packed them with slabs of a hard rubbery material called gutta percha, made from latex obtained from the gutta-percha tree in Malaya.

Pieces of this hard rubbery material fell into the hands of a curious London golfer, who discovered it had plastic qualities and could be moulded into shapes if softened in hot water. In due course crude golf balls were made from gutta percha and were the subject of many experiments.

The first 'gutties', as they came to be called, were smooth and had disappointing characteristics, tending to drop suddenly to earth after flying a few yards. It was noticed that a well-used ball flew better than a new one, but when restored to smoothness, by immersion in hot water, behaved badly the next day. Obviously the cuts and dents inflicted in the guttie in the course of play provided the necessary air resistance which, in the case of the featherie, had derived from the stitched seams. The guttie experimenters therefore hammered lines and indentations all round the newly made balls. And before long patterned moulds were evolved by which regular designs were impressed during manufacture.

The makers of feather balls were aghast at this new production but soon had to capitulate. Here was a ball practically indestructable which cost much less to make than the featherie, and could be renovated or remade time after time by a simple do-it-yourself process. This caused a revolution in the world of golf which during the next few years rapidly extended its territories and greatly increased its population. The guttie in various forms reigned for half a century during which many courses were laid out in England and other parts of the world outside Scotland. And golf, from being a pastime of the idle rich, became a popular sport with the well-to-do business and middle classes.

During this period, too, the Open and Amateur Championships were instituted, and the ground prepared for the big commercial exploitation of golf which, a century after the introduction of the guttie, was to reach heights undreamed of by the Victorian pioneers. The Open Championship began in an extremely modest way in 1860, when some members of the Prestwick Golf Club subscribed for a challenge belt and six Scottish professionals competed over three rounds of the Prestwick links, which then consisted of only 12 holes. Willie Park of Musselburgh was the first winner of the Belt and the first prize of, it is believed, £5, and Tom Morris of St. Andrews was second. These two outstanding players continued their rivalry over the next few years with varying fortunes, until in 1868 Young Tommy Morris, son of Tom, became Champion Golfer. He won also in 1869 and 1870 and by these three successive wins made the Belt his own property.

For one year the championship lapsed. Then, a cup having been subscribed for by members of the Prestwick, Honourable Company and Royal and Ancient clubs, the series was resumed. Young Tommy won for the fourth successive year, a record which stands to this day, and no doubt he would have won many more times had not death cut short the career of a man who, it would appear from his scores, was years ahead of his time in skill and competitive power.

The Cup, being a perpetual trophy, is still with us, but there has been a profound change in the character and scope of the Open Championship. In the days of the Parks and the Morrises it was a small almost local competition confined to a few men who, having taken to golf as caddies, had progressed to a point where they could earn small sums of money by playing the game, to supplement their incomes from clubmaking. Today the same Cup is played for by men who earn in many cases five-figure incomes, the best of whom are not far short of the millionaire class and have very little if anything to do with the activities of a club professional. And the first prize represents a four-hundredfold increase on that 1860 first prize of £5, although still dwarfed by other big prizes given in the biggest and most elaborate commercial tournaments on both sides of the Atlantic.

The match-play event which each year decides who shall be known as the Champion Amateur Golfer also had a humble start. In 1885 the Royal Liverpool Golf Club organized an open match-play tournament for amateurs which was won by A. F. MacFie. This was so successful that the Hoylake golfers proposed to other clubs in England and Scotland the institution of an Amateur Championship, and this was inaugurated in 1886. Many years afterwards the Royal and Ancient decided to include the 1885 competition in the records, and MacFie was canonized as the first Champion Amateur Golfer. By this date (1920) national championships of all kinds were in existence in the United States, where golf had been introduced in 1888, and the Continent of Europe, as well as in English-speaking countries overseas; and between the world wars the golf calendar was further embellished with various international contests, paramount being the Ryder Cup for professionals and the Walker Cup for amateurs.

But to go back to the nineteenth century, the last dozen years of which saw the real development of golf from the esoteric pastime of the few to a sport for the masses. Business men in our big cities took up the game. It became a fashionable adjunct of suburban pursuits, and, under the influence of property speculators, golf courses sprang up like mushrooms, not always on the most suitable terrain, but undoubtedly meeting an ever-increasing demand from the city worker seeking a readily accessible means of 're-creating tired tissues'.

With this widening of interest in golf came publicity for its great players and such men as Harry Vardon, J. H. Taylor, James Braid, Sandy Herd and Ted Ray became internationally famous. Vardon went to the United States for a tour in 1900, won the U.S. Open Championship, and created an enthusiasm for the game which was to produce pupils who surpassed the masters—the Bobby Joneses and Walter Hagens of the 1920s and the Arnold Palmers and Jack Nicklauses of the 1960s. It is problematical if the horizons which opened up for golf in the early days of the twentieth century would have appeared but for one all-important catalyst—the rubber-cored ball. For 50 years up to the death of Queen Victoria golfers had used the comparatively unresponsive solid guttie which required a deal of forcing along, and had to be very well struck indeed to give satisfactory results. Then, with the turn of the century, all this was changed. Experiments had been carried on for some time in Britain and the United States in the attempt to achieve a more resilient ball, and in 1902 Dr. Haskell, an American, introduced one with a rubber core and a gutta-percha cover. The early Haskells bore little resemblance to the modern ball. They lacked the durability of the guttie and were more costly. But in theory they had undeniable advantages, and the death of the guttie was hastened by the fact that Sandy Herd won the Open of 1902 at Hoylake using a Haskell ball. Everyone wanted the new ball and prices were high for a time, but new supplies, improved methods of manufacture, and the adoption of the rubber-core principle by British firms, soon achieved economic stability and converted the guttie into a museum-piece.

The importance of the rubber-core revolution was that it came at a critical period in golf development. The growing popularity of the game demanded an easier means of playing it. For the beginner the guttie ball meant a painful and frustrating initiation into the mysteries of the game. It flew well only when well struck, and if mis-hit would not only find trouble but also sting the hands of the tyro. The rubber-core on the other hand, with its lively, rubber-wound body, was much easier on the hands and more responsive to an unskilful stroke. True, its greater liveliness and length meant, perhaps, more trouble for the slicer or the hooker, but the feeblest blow would send it bounding along, and even when topped it would achieve a creditable distance except when stopped in mid-career by the then fashionable cross-bunkers.

One notable effect of the increasing popularity of golf was the demand for improvements in the design and character of golf clubs. For many years hickory had been the standard wood for shafts, and persimmon for club-heads, both originating in the United States. As the demand for equipment grew supplies of good hickory became scarce, and in 1926 America legalized steel shafts. The Royal and Ancient followed suit in 1930, and now that materials were of constant quality it was possible to standardize manufacture and evolve the 'matched set'.

In recent years plastic materials have come into increasing use for the manufacture of 'wooden' club-heads, and with other modern embellishments, such as the use of stainless steel and chromium steel for the heads of iron clubs, and coloured plastic material for golf bags, the mid-century golfer enjoys the best of everything. He is one of many millions who play their beloved game in almost every civilized part of the globe. He is the heir of the Parks and the Morrises, who once hit feather-stuffed balls with rudely spliced play-clubs, but gave us a wonderful heritage. Golf is ultra-modern and universal, but only the techniques and the environment of the game has changed, not its spirit.

It is still 'a science, in which you may exhaust yourself, but never your subject'. These well-known words might well form the text for this book, which, in rhyme and reason, sense and nonsense, has culled from present and past many of the literary and artistic gems which golf has provided over a century or more.

'Thou art a gentle sprite. We owe thee much' were the concluding sentences of the first-known book on golf. And they will be echoed in the hearts of millions of golfers in the four quarters of the globe who now play the game which, when those words were written, was scarcely known outside Scotland, its home.

The Unique 'Old Course'

By George Duncan

I F I AM asked which is my favourite course I give my answer unhesitatingly—the Old Course at St. Andrews. I think it is the best, and if I have got to play a match which is really of some importance that is where I want to play it. St. Andrews has got a character and features that you find nowhere else. What I like about it is this, that you may play a very good shot there and find yourself in a very bad place. That is the real game of golf. I don't want everything levelled and smoothed away so that by no possible chance can your ball take an unlucky turn in a direction you don't like. People think and talk too much about 'fairness'.

Keep your Eye on the Ball

By Arnold Haultain

I F THAT all-important little rule, 'Keep your Eye on the Ball', means anything at all, it means keep it on the ball so that the ball is distinctly seen and attended to. One should watch one's ball as a cat watches a mouse. No cat watches a mouse with downcast eyes or with a vacant stare; and no cat, while it watches a mouse, is thinking of anything else.

Golf is more exacting than racing, cards, speculation or matrimony. Golf gives no margin : either you win or you fail. You cannot hedge; you cannot bluff; you cannot give a stop-order; you cannot jilt. One chance is given you, and you hit or miss. There is nothing more rigid in life. And it is this ultra and extreme rigidity that makes golf so intensely interesting.

In almost all other games you pit yourself against a mortal foe; in golf it is yourself against the world : no human being stays your progress as you drive your ball over the face of the globe.

Bobby Jones's Year

By Frank Moran

A MONG years in golf that should have the distinction of extra large red letters, surely 1930 is one. It was supremely dominated by an American, but it will shine for all time in the records of our championships. It was Bobby Jones's year, when he did the almost unbelievable thing by winning four national championships in a row— the British Amateur and Open, and the corresponding titles in his own country. This was Jones's last Open, for he retired on the peak of that great year. He was then aged twenty-eight.

Winding Up for the Stroke[1]

By John Jacobs

WHAT do we want from the back-swing? Simply this : that at the top of it the body, arms and hands are in a position to swing the club into the back of the ball.

The right wind-up makes it easy for the arms to hit straight through in the right plane of swing.

That is absolutely all we are aiming at.

Let's now look at what is involved—and where so many golfers make things difficult for themselves.

(i) The First Movement of the Swing

Leaving aside for the moment the waggle or waggles—the little dummy movements of swing in miniature which help any player to get himself relaxed and ready for the stroke—the first movement of the easy golf swing is the thing called the *Forward Press*.

It is, I want to emphasize, an integral part of *Swinging*.

It is bound up with the mechanics of the easiest way of beginning any movement. Most readers will know of the old trick whereby when you have a heavy weight to lift, if you begin by first pressing hard down on it, and then lift straight up, out of the 'press,' the load seems to come up more easily.

This is nothing to do with the effect upon the weight itself. It is everything to do with the effect of the 'press' on your own muscles. It is like the similar technique we all use to move a stationary car by hand, when we first ease it imperceptibly back, the better to start it forwards.

The Forward Press is, in fact, a slight easing of body and hands into the beginning of the reverse wind-up in the back-swing.

It is also, and not entirely incidentally, a small reminder, or re-hearsal-note, for the fore-swing itself, which is going to develop in turn out of the back-swing. Its general job, in fact, is to help the whole swing on the way.

1. From *Golf* by John Jacobs (Stanley Paul).

One of Britain's best,
Peter Butler in play in
the World Match Play
Tournament at
Wentworth

Tony Lema, winner of
the 1964 British Open
Championship,
practising his wedge
shot

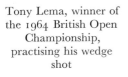

Dai Rees advocates indoor practice in the winter. The exercise (*above*) helps to improve a player's touch

The mirror test. Rees looks through the looking-glass to see that his head remains stationary during a putt

Nearly every player has a forward press of some sort or another, whether he knows it or not, since it is extremely difficult to begin the back-swing from nothing. But it remains a difficult thing to teach, in that it is so personal to each player.

In most cases it means turning the body slightly to the left (the follow-through side) so as to get a running start at the back-swing. What I want to stress here is that it is worth paying some attention to, if only to make sure that the movement into the back-swing is continuous.

The back-swing actually starts with the forward press; after which this little swing forward of the body, arms and hands (though not the club-head), reverses in steady rhythm into the swing itself.

(ii) *Winding up—in Plane*

I think the back-swing is best described, and thought of, as a *swinging wrist-cock*.

You don't lift up the club; your body and shoulders wind up, quite naturally and smoothly, as you swing the club back and round and up until the limit of shoulder-turn is reached, and the momentum of the club-head pulls your wrists into their full-cocked hitting position.

Golf is a game of controlled tension, not sloppy relaxation. If the back-swing is right, we shall feel tightly wound like strong elastic, and therefore ready to deliver the blow at the ball.

A feeling of winding up the spine and muscles, while hanging on to the ground with the feet and legs, is what we are looking for. The left heel may be dragged off the ground at the top of the back-swing; *but as the shoulders wind up until the back is facing the target—the legs should be resisting this turn.*

There must be *resistance* in the back-swing; something for it to wind-up against, and which is ready to start unwinding it again as soon as you give the word.

The better the wind-up, the less we have to worry about that old object of attention, the left arm. Golf is very largely centrifugal, and therefore if we really wind up properly, the left arm will stay reasonably straight; it should not be rigidly stiffened anyway.

That being so, whether one arrives at the top of the back-swing with a straight (but not necessarily flat) left wrist, or with one which is cocked under the shaft, is not important. You can be a thoroughly good player from either of these positions at the top.

Now, how about all the old problems of hip-turn, pivot, shoulder turn, and the relationship of hands and club-head to the rest of the back-swing, about which so many week-end golfers get themselves

G

really bothered and worried? Luckily, there is a general guiding solution to all of them, and I am going to suggest it now; it is the *plane* of the swing.

It is not in the least difficult to discover your own plane, and work on it. When you are addressing the ball correctly, the plane of your swing for that shot is that set by an imaginary straight line coming up from the ball, resting on top of your shoulders and continuing beyond them. The easiest way to see this is to look in a mirror. Stand as if you were driving directly away from it, then practise swinging back the club in such a way that as you look at it in the mirror the club-head never leaves that ball-shoulders line, and ends in a position still in line with it above the shoulders.

If you can get this idea of the plane of the swing, then it is very easy to get the correct shoulder pivot, the right amount of hip-turn, and—very important—the correct relationship between the hands and the club-head.

For a simple example, see how if you drag the club-head straight back from the ball along the floor, with the hands leading too much, it at once goes *outside* the plane-line; while if you roll it back with a turn of the forearms, so that the club-head leads too much, it at once goes *inside* it. It should do neither of these things; it should swing back in line (or, more correctly, 'in plane') with the plane-line at every point.

Let's look closely at where this gets us.

First: at the top of the full back-swing, the club-shaft should be pointing at the target (approximately—individuals must vary slightly), with both hands and club in plane. This is just how you want them, so that as you begin to unwind again into the down-swing, the hands start off swinging the club back in the right direction back down through the swing-plane to hit the ball.

Second: taking the swing of the club back to this point automatically ensures just about the right amount of pivot and wrist action, pulling against the anchor of the legs and feet.

Third: the winding-up movement can take the club-head most easily up in plane all the time, if the head and spine are kept still. They must be, and the swing must be wound-up *around* them, with no lifting or swaying—in fact in the simplest movement possible.

Fourth: you can see at once that as far as the pivot is concerned (that is, the winding around of the body and shoulders until the back of the shoulders face the hole while the club-head above them points in precisely the same direction) there is bound to be a shoulder movement intermediate between tilting them and merely turning them.

'By golly, you're right—he *has* dropped off.'

In other words, there is bound to be some shoulder-tilt, and some shoulder-turn.

These two must be balanced in the right combination if the back-swing is to go back 'in plane;' and it is when they get out of balance with each other, as they very easily and very often do with very many players, that the swing leaves its own plane and the correct relationship between hands and club-head is lost.

(iii) *How Things go Wrong*

Let's take a look at how things do go wrong. This is really common sense; but observation in the mirror will help to make it even clearer. If the shoulders 'tilt' too much, that is if they turn in too much of a vertical plane, then the whole swing will be lifted above the ball-to-shoulder line, and what we call a 'too-upright' swing will result.

If, on the other hand, the shoulders 'turn' too much, that is revolve in too much of a horizontal plane, then the swing will be pulled down under the ball-to-shoulder line, and will be 'flat.'

Too much tilt: swing too upright. Too much turn: swing too flat.

Now this is important, and I think helpful; because any variation here, on either side of what I call the normal ball-to-shoulder swing-plane, has marked effects upon the ensuing relationship between club-head, arms and body.

In the too-upright swing (too much tilt, too little turn) the hands usually lead the club-head back above (or outside) the normal swing-plane-line, and the right elbow flies out like a chicken's wing at the top of the back-swing. The result is loss of control and an action too steep to get into the back of the ball easily—as the club swings too sharply up and down. People who do this very often have a tendency to hit the ground, to top, pull or slice. (Yes, all these things!)

Conversely, the flat swing (too little tilt, too much turn) is usually combined with an early roll-over of the wrists, so that the club-head leads the back-swing *under* (or inside) the ball-to-shoulder swing-plane. People who do this often arrive at the top of the back-swing with the right elbow almost *locked* to the right side under the shoulder, so that they tend to throw that right arm and shoulder outside at the beginning of the down-swing, thus causing topping, hooking, pushing, fluffing and socketing!

It really is much easier to play the game with a back-swing kept, as closely as is comfortable for you, to that ball-to-shoulder plane.

The best back-swings *are*, in practice, 'in plane;' and, I repeat, they automatically set up the correct relationship between the hands and the club-head.

They also help tremendously to keep the club-face 'square' to the target throughout the swing—which is the easiest way of hitting the ball straight. 'Square' merely means in the same relationship to the hands and arms as it was at the address position, when you carefully aimed it at the target.

Both variations from the ball-to-shoulder plane have a complicating effect upon the aiming of the club-face at impact. The upright swing will make the blade 'shut' (that is, to the left of its correct position) on the way back from the ball and then cross over on the way up and lie 'open' (the reverse twist) at the top. The flat swing will tend to 'open' the blade at first, but will cross it over on the way up to make it 'shut' at the top.

You can check which you are doing yourself in the mirror. If the blade or face has stayed 'square' it will be lying, at the top of the back-swing, approximately in line with and parallel to the ball-to-shoulder plane line. If the toe of the club-head points across towards the horizon, though, then the blade is shut; and if the toe points downwards towards the ground, then it is open.

From either of these latter positions you can hit the ball straight. I think, though, that—especially if either comes from a too-upright or too-flat back-swing—they make golf a little more difficult. But there can be no rules exact for every player.

(iv) *How far, How fast, Where?*

What more remains to the simple factors governing the easiest and most reliable back-swing?

There's WEIGHT, of course. Golfers used once to be taught to transfer their weight consciously on to the right foot during the back-swing—a sort of slight sway sideways from the ball. I'm against this. I think there had far better be no *conscious* transfer of weight at all, but what you should concentrate on is keeping to that feeling you should have at the address of resting on a tall shooting stick. You should still be thus slightly 'sitting down' at the top of the back-swing, with the shoulders and hands completely wound up. You should certainly never thrust your weight back on to a rigid straight right leg (nor, for that matter, forward on to the left).

What about SPEED? That's another old arguing point. So often one hears 'Slow back!' But one can go back too slowly, with the club not actually being *swung* back at all. I sometimes feel that the so-called 'one-piece method' has been taken too far and has caused artificial slowness on the back-swing. We all have our own speeds, in actual fact. I couldn't swing at the speed of Charlie Ward, and I don't suppose he could swing at my more leisurely pace. But in both our cases our body, hand and arm actions are synchronized into a rhythm which suits us individually—for size, for temperament and for the way we are put together.

A player must find his or her own speed—so long as it is rhythmic, and—I repeat—leads to a swinging wrist-cock which winds up the body, hands and arms together.

Much the same goes for the LENGTH of the swing. We all have our different length of swing, due to varying flexibility of body and wrists, and the way we let our wrists cock naturally at the end of the back-swing. The best measure of what is right for any one of us is this: that our proper length of swing is the one we naturally get back to with the shoulders fully turned, the head still, *both* hands still firmly in control of the club, the left arm reasonably straight and the left heel not pulled too high off the ground. I am of the opinion that most people's swings are too long simply because one or more of these points is at fault.

All this amounts to the fact that the swing must be properly full, but never to the point where the lower part of the body 'gives in' during the back-swing and lets go of the sure grip of leg and foot upon the ground.

What makes a back-swing *too short*, on the other hand, is any failure to reach a full shoulder-turn. The full shoulder-turn is essential to aim the whole swing at the target, and lack of it will almost always throw us outside the proper arc, to come out-to-in at the ball and much too easily pull it straight to the left, or slice it curving to the right.

(v) *Words always in Season*

When I am teaching, I continually find myself using some phrases over and over again to player after player. Since these would seem to be the ones I have found most helpful to the most players, it may be worth repeating them yet once more. They are :

1. 'Don't lift up : wind up.'
2. 'Start the back-swing with the right shoulder getting out of the way.'
3. 'Point the club-head at the target in the back-swing.' (This, incidentally, is a quick way of getting a beginner to pivot, and to cock the wrists.)
4. 'As near as possible, keep your feet flat on the ground.'
5. 'Stay "sat down" as you turn your shoulders.'

One last thought, which may ring a bell with one or two readers, I think golf is very akin to baseball—in this way : in baseball a player swings in plane with the flight of the ball as it comes towards him. In golf, all we have to do is to swing in plane with however far away we are from the ball—which partly depends on what club we are using. For any shot and any club, the plane most likely to be easiest really is that ranging straight up from the ball just over the shoulders, as you stand to address it for the shot.

Momentum into the Shot[1]

By John Jacobs

I have described the back-swing both as a 'wind-up' and as a 'swinging wrist-cock;' both of them within your own plane of swing—which extends from the ball straight up over your shoulders as you stand at the address.

Now, how to let both the wind-up and the swinging wrist-cock reverse themselves naturally into an effective golf stroke?

What is wanted is a reversal of what you did on the back-swing. But it is not a simple one. Two things are different.

One is that although you want to unwind, and swing, back into the correct position you took up at the address, you are not going to slow down and stop there. On the contrary, your swing is going to generate an increasing momentum all the way down until your club-head reaches its maximum speed (for that particular stroke) as it brings the club-face into the ball and on through the position where it lay.

The second is that the order of the unwinding movement of different parts of your body is not the exact reversal of their order in the wind-up.

For instance, the last thing that happened on the back-swing was the completion of that swinging wrist-cock, with the momentum of the club pulling your wrists into the cocked position. About the worst thing to do is to reverse that as the first movement of the down-swing. On the contrary, you want to save that unleashing of the hands for hitting the ball.

While the back-swing builds up to a position of potential, where movement stops and then reverses direction, the down-swing unleashes itself progressively into movement at top speed, discharging that potential into the ball.

(i) Starting Down

The correct start down begins in the lower half of the body—the legs and the hips. That is why telling people to 'stay sat down' in the

1. From *Golf* by John Jacobs (Stanley Paul).

back-swing, and to 'get the left heel down first' in the down-swing, is often good advice; doing so consolidates the anchor point of the feet, and starts the hips swinging back into and through the address position. This automatically begins to pull on the arms and hands and unwind them towards the ball.

Just as the swinging wrist-cock of the back-swing *ended* with the actual cocking of the wrists, so the swinging uncock of the down-swing *ends* with the uncocking of the wrists, as you unleash the power of your hands into the stroke.

(ii) *Shoulders Back*

The commonest bad shots are undoubtedly caused by the shoulders getting out of sequence! Although they obviously take their natural place in the general unwinding from the back-swing, they do not swing past the ball ahead of the hands, as the hips do. They unwind towards the ball, but it is the hands and arms which swing and direct the club-head through the ball, in complete partnership with the hips. The hands and arms, then, swing the club-head ahead of the shoulders, while *they* more slowly complete their revolution right through to the follow-through. On the follow-through, in fact, it is the momentum of the club-head, through the hands, which pulls them round to the finish.

The commonest fault in golf, then, is the shoulders getting out of sequence, so that instead of reversing that swinging wrist-cock, the player begins to hit right from the top of the back-swing *with his shoulders*.

Although this is one form of 'hitting early,' it directly causes a hit 'too late' with the hands, simply because (in many players at any rate) hitting too early with the shoulders carries the hands through the ball before they have had time fully to unleash their uncocking action at it. The usual result is that the club-face doesn't have time to swing back square to the ball, makes contact still open and a slice results.

This is often made worse by the fact that the man who hits early with his shoulders usually also rolls them horizontally at the same time, so that the right shoulder comes *round* instead of *under* his chin, and so that his swing is thrown outside the proper arc on the way down, to cut across the ball from outside to in.

This takes us straight back, I think, to the easiest way of hitting the ball straight!

To hit the ball straight, all we need at impact is a square blade and a swing on line and in plane.

(iii) *Hitting Straight*

The beginner, and he who aims to improve his game, must have faith here. He must believe something quite simple: that there is no need to do any conscious squaring up of the blade in the down-swing, or in the hitting area, with the hands! The hands should be left free for hitting the ball. The correct down-swing action from the top, in the correct sequence, will take care of the blade of the club as it swings through the ball.

It really does all depend upon how the body is wound up and unwound. The hands and arms need to swing freely from the hub of the wind-up. Wind-up, then unwind, and swing the club-head while you are doing this by a free use of the hands and arms.

This type of action works for every club in the bag, allowing the loft on each to do the work as necessary.

(iv) *Hitting Clean*

We need to be in plane to hit the ball cleanly.

The swing must come back in the right arc to match the player's address position. He must be hitting the ball with the club-head attacking from somewhere behind the shot, as it were; but his club-head must neither be approaching it at too steep an angle, nor at an angle too close along the ground.

If the club-head comes in too steeply, he will tend either to chop down on the ball, or to hit it on its top with the club-head still on the way to the bottom of the swing. On the other hand, if the club-head comes in on an arc too flat along the ground, he will be liable to fluff the shot by hitting the ground behind the ball, or else to top the ball, this time by catching it with the bottom edge of his club already on its way up, after passing through the bottom point of its arc.

The swing mistakes which cause these more difficult approaches to the ball are as follows: hitting too late with the wrists and hands, thus steepening the club-head's arc into a last-moment dive attack on it; and hitting too early with the wrists and hands, thus flattening the swing along the ground before it gets to the ball.

Do note this, though: the wrist action in the hitting area is very closely bound up with the general aim and action of the swing. If the stance and swing so far have been square, that is, correctly aimed at the target, then the hands can follow a normal action and hit the ball straight. But if the stance and/or swing has been aimed markedly to the right, then the hands and wrists will end to roll in the hitting area; while if the general aim or swing has been to the left, the wrist and hand action will tend to 'block' in the hitting area.

Both these variations make golf more difficult!

(v) *Getting the Left Side out of the Way*

You may have heard quite a bit about 'hitting against the left side.' I don't say that that is never good advice. But it does depend on who you are, and how you naturally swing. For the player who opens the face of the club at the top of the back-swing, the idea of hitting against the left side can help; in order to hit the ball straight, he has to roll his hands and wrists into the hitting area, and the idea of hitting against the left side will help him to do this.

For most people, though, I think it is better and more reliable advice to think of 'getting the left side out of the way' in the hitting area. If you do this, you make more room for the arms and hands to come through. Though still allowing the full application of wrist-power into the shot, getting the left side out of the way slows down any tendency to roll the wrists (right over left) as the power is applied, and thus makes it easier to swing the club-face squarely through the ball and on into the follow-through.

Most good players do clear the left side out of the way before the actual stroke, *but their shoulders still await their turn in the swing,* with the right shoulder then swinging *under* the chin and not *out and round.*

People who 'tense up' at the mere sight of a ball, again, can still often be helped by being told to hit against the left side—merely because it can be one way of stopping them from turning their shoulders right from the top of the back-swing—a habit we were talking about just now.

To many people this getting the left side to swing clear, out of the way, so that hand and arm action can come through unrestricted while the right shoulder is still swinging under the chin, is the most difficult part of the game. 'Hips out of the way and right shoulder under' describes, to me, very much the feel of the down and through swing, however. This allows the whole of the right side to come into the shot *behind* the hit, giving, incidentally, maximum power and momentum, and an easy sweep on into a full follow-through.

(vi) *From Impact to Follow-through*

In the good golf swing, there must be freedom. Not just that which comes naturally from getting the left side out of the way, so that the right side can swing through after the ball and into the full finish, but also that from a sensible use of the head.

Certainly, you want to keep your head still until the ball is struck and away; but any attempt to glue it down to the bitter end is going to restrict your action through the hitting area, and cut down the free follow-through which should follow.

The effects of that will carry right back into the actual stroke, and you will lose both power and accuracy. If the stroke is anticipating a spavined follow-through, it will also anticipate, in its own action, some of the same weakness. The golf swing and the actual stroke alike demand freedom if they are to fulfil themselves naturally and completely.

As long as the hit is under (by which I mean very much like a straight bat in cricket), the swinging of the left hip out of the way will allow for complete freedom of hitting with the right hand without any fear of rolling the club-face.

(vii) *The Ladies Differ*

Incidentally, for ladies the down-swing does tend to be slightly different. Even the best of them usually begin to uncock the wrists earlier in the down-swing than men need to, in order to reach maximum speed at impact. This is simply because their wrists and hands are not as strong as men's are. Consequently, since the club-head widens its arc into the ball, due to this earlier straightening of the wrists, many of the leading ladies tend to come up on to their toes at impact, simply in order to make room for their wider club-head arc to get into the ball without hitting the ground first. By coming up on to the toes they give their club-head that much more room to swing cleanly forward into and through the ball.

(viii) *Individuals Vary*

This brings us back to one of the most important things in any attempt to help other people with their golf—including this one!

Discussing simple sound general principles is one thing: teaching and applying them to particular individuals is quite another. And because there is no one distinct way of playing and swinging, the written word can never be as effective as the lesson from a competent professional.

Any good swing must balance individual variations within itself. To take two extreme examples: swinging with a blade shut at the top of the back-swing may call for coming through with hips turning more towards the hole at impact than usual; while swinging with a blade open at the top may call for much more of the feeling of hitting against a firm left side.

The good instructor will not normally—in my opinion, anyway—tamper with the things a player does naturally. For instance, it does not matter whether the wrists are under the shaft at the top of the back-swing or not—so long as the blade is brought back to square in the hitting area. The whole movement of any individual's swing has to be balanced to give a square blade and a straight-through swing at impact—in the simplest fashion *for that person.*

That is one more reason why—again in my opinion—the keen week-end golfer should seek, and take, much more advice from his club professional than he or she usually does.

(ix) *The Usefulness of Practising*

When talking of practice, here, I am assuming that the reader plays just for pleasure, and has neither taste nor time for practising on the scale and with the determination a young professional needs to forge his game.

I personally love practising. I love experimenting, which probably helps my teaching—if not my playing! I have discovered, though, that if I find myself practising badly, I must stop for a little while and try to re-create a simple mental picture of exactly what I am trying to do.

This need for a mental picture, of course, goes right through all golf. We must have it every time, both of the execution of each shot, and also of the flight of the ball. We must see in our mind's eye exactly what we are just about to do. This is particularly important in short shots, where we must picture both the flight and the roll required. The same goes for the putt; we must picture the line and how the rolling ball will take any borrow.

In practising your full golf swing, you want to rely, to begin with, on the mental picture your instructor will have given you—of how *you* can best swing the club. Your practising to learn this swing can mainly be done with one club. A 6-iron, for instance, is fairly easy to use; but the stroke with it contains all the ingredients of a full swing. What you need is pure repetition of the mental picture given, and—so long as you do not begin to lose interest—as much of it as is needed to get the swing completely right and repetitive.

Most of the world's leading players have done this, at the stage of their 'grooving' period, even if later in their careers they reserve more of their energy for actual competition—as do nowadays Locke, Thomson and others who very rarely play more than 18 holes practice in one day. At their stage, where their swings have settled down, they need just short spells, going right through the bag of clubs one by one, to keep the rhythm and the swing ticking over.

All through your life, though, the short game—the 'feel' part of the game—needs constant attention if it is to keep up to your best standard. This is a lesson I might as well teach myself; for I find, now that I spend so much time teaching, that although my long game

'I'll be off then . . .

seems to stay put, chipping and pitching quickly leave me if I don't
keep practising them.

Obviously, too, time spent practising putting is time well spent.
We have always been taught that the putting stroke should be a
smooth one. But this is not enough in itself. The gentle stuff, with lots
of follow-through, is fine if the putting surface is perfect. But with
anything less than a perfect surface, the stroke must have more
authority.

(x) *Keeping Golf in its Right Place*

Golf being the difficult game that it is, it is very easy for any of us to lose our sense of proportion about it. I seem to meet far too many people who regard as a disaster of the first magnitude a couple of fluffed pitches or a drive into the rough. In point of fact, of course, the greatest players hit very few shots completely as they intend to; and I think it does much for our temperament in golf if we realize and accept this. I often want to say to one of my pupils : 'Who are you to think you can do more than they can!'

If golf is a difficult game, however, we should all be the more grateful for our good shots. After all, the game is tougher than any of us—and will always win. The best players will follow a sparkling 64 with a puzzled 75; or will win a tournament one week—and fail to qualify the next!

Try hard we must—but we must also keep a sense of proportion!

The Caddy Knew Best[1]

T HE accomplishment of a hole in one has called forth a variety of comments from caddies. This happened in Scotland.

After the argument that seems inevitable when Southern players are attended by Scottish caddies the golfer had decided to take his No. 3 iron at a short hole, the caddie protesting to the end that the shot required a spoon.

Having duly made his 'ace', the golfer turned and said : 'There you are—you were wrong, you see. A No. 3 was all that was wanted.'

'Ye dommed fool,' said the caddie. 'Ye should have took the spoon. Yon shot will cost ye a poond !'

On another occasion it was a London golfer who performed the feat. After a great deal of argument and not a little acrimony he had decided on an iron club against the advice of his caddie. In went the ball and 'There you are !' he cried triumphantly.

'Yes,' said the caddie, 'but you'd have done better with a spoon.'

1. From *Candid Caddies.*

The Self-made Man

By Henry Longhurst

To scale the heights in the profession Cotton chose for himself a man requires two assets—a tough physique and an icy control of his emotions. Cotton had neither. The Cotton of today is the perfect example of the self-made man. He 'made' his mind and he 'made' his body. . . .

His battle with his 'temperament' is an interesting study to the man on the touchline, who doesn't have to endure the mental agonies of the player wrestling with the turbulent emotions that surge within him. . . .

Cotton, unlike Hagen, sought complete perfection. Where Hagen, admitting the fallibility of the human make-up, expected four of five execrable shots per round—and made them—Cotton regarded every imperfect stroke as a personal failure. A short putt missed meant, for him, the tortures of the damned. He used to strike himself on the head, quite hard, with his own putter !

I suppose the secret was—and it was certainly part of the secret of his main success—that he was keen on golf, keener than any man in Great Britain.

Below: In 1938 Denys Scott wore large checked plus fours and waterproof jacket

Above: The changing fashions of golf. Abe Mitchell, with buttoned jacket in 1929

This is one way of finding
out if the hole ahead is clear

'Hoisting the Body' at
Blundellsands Golf Club

At the Swilcan Burn[1]

By Andrew Kirkaldy

WE LADS used to play golf—either a real game or else just driving about a ball, or putting at some hole—in those days almost constantly when there was no carrying to be done, and one of my first recollections about the game is that there always was a great scarcity of golf balls. We often, not having a ball at all, would hold putting competitions—for pennies, of course—at some hole, either old corks or else small round stones doing duty instead; and I can tell you we often used to have to run for it from old Davie Honeyman, the greenkeeper, although, of course, he was not an old man then, for this. But he would generally leave us alone if we were putting with real golf balls, which he thought did not destroy the putting greens so much—so he said, at least—as the corks and stones.

At that time, and for many a year afterwards, until the present strict links by-laws were made and enforced, the boys down there would often, when in want of a ball, take to dirtying the water of the Swilcan Burn by wading in it, and thus stirring up the mud, so that any balls which might be driven into it were almost always lost—to their real owners, at least. I am afraid I must confess to having been guilty of this, along with the other boys of my own time; and when I have said so much I might as well also describe what our particular method of carrying this out was—namely, to sit well under the lee of the old stone bridge there, out of sight, and puddle up the mud of the burn either with our feet or with sticks, so sending down the stream water which was quite thick and muddy, and then woe betide any ball that went there, at least until the mud had settled or passed, when there was a slight chance of seeing it. But for this most players had not the time or patience to wait, and so we would thus manage occasionally to secure a ball.

Honeyman, as I have said before, was not so angry with us for playing about on a putting green when we did it with a real ball, although if he had only known where the balls sometimes came from, and how we got them into our possession, he might have been angrier still; but probably he had a pretty good idea, all the same.

1. From *Great Golfers in the Making* (Methuen).

Playing For Coppers[1]

By *Alexander Herd*

(Open Champion, 1902)

LONG before the time came when I was the proud possessor of some real golf clubs I and my boy friends, feeling that we must play golf of some sort, used to go out into the woods to look for 'shunties,' as we used to call them. They were those parts of suitable trees which were eminently adapted for the purpose of making fairly respectable clubs, and the heads that we fashioned in this way were not at all bad. Real golf balls, of course, were far beyond us, and the substitutes that we adopted were not balls at all, but champagne corks, and we used to search for them at the back of the brae where the rubbish from the hotels and other places was thrown.

It was not on the links, but in North Street, where I was born, that I played what, by considerably stretching the meaning of the word, might be called my first game of golf. We played from the 'wee wyndie' to Bell Street, and from Bell Street back to the 'wee wyndie,' this making up one 'round;' while the lamp-posts, which we had to hit with our champagne corks, stood for the holes. Oh! we little chaps had some great games in the 'wee wyndie.' Most of us were only about seven or eight years old. Some were destined to do well in golf when we grew up.

My own bosom friend was Laurence Auchterlonie, or 'Laurie,' as we all called him then and do still. We were always together, and we grew up in golf side by side, telling each other day by day the thoughts and dreams that we had of winning medals and cups and getting high up in the championship some time when we were older, and had clubs and balls, and could drive like the great players of that time could do. Laurie eventually went out to America, and in due course he won the American Championship, so that our respective ambitions have been fairly realized.

With the boys the big market at St. Andrews in August was kept as a kind of festival, and then Laurie and I would go scavenging for

1. From *Great Golfers in the Making* (Methuen).

balls among the whins. You can't lose balls at St. Andrews in these days, but there were plenty lost when we were boys, and those that we found we did not keep and play with—they were far too valuable for that—but sold them to Forgan. In the same way our commercial instinct prompted us to go out to the targets and pick up all the lead that we could find, and this we used to sell to Forgan for weighting clubs.

Laurence Auchterlonie was a better player than I was in those days, but he took the game up as a profession later than I did. Of course, we soon wanted something better than the golf in North Street, and we toddled away to the links like a dog would go to the water, for there seemed to be no other place to go to. And if we little chaps were judged very strictly we were professionals from the very start, for as soon as we had any coppers of our own we played golf against each other for them. Five or six of us would organize a little competition, and there would be a prize of threepence for the first, twopence for the second and a penny for the third. Such golf as we played had our undivided allegiance. Occasionally we had a game of rugby football, but practically there was only one game in the world so far as we were concerned.

My mother was our club repairer. She used to stick on the heads for us with an old gutty ball melted down, or occasionally used glue. She had a very worried time when the heads came off, particularly as I had three young brothers at home at that time who all needed similar service from her.

I well remember the circumstances by which I came into possession of the first real golf club that I ever owned. I was somewhere about nine years of age at the time, and my father had been looking kindly upon my enthusiasm for the game and my boyish desire to do well at it. I had been worrying him for a long time to get me a club made, but he said that clubs were scarce, and it seemed to be his desire that they should remain so. But my appeals at last had effect, and one glorious day my father told me to come along with him to get the club that I wanted. Never was I happier than I was that day. He took me down to the shop of poor Jamie Anderson, the champion player, who died not long ago. Ben Laing was working for him as a clubmaker at that time, and it was Ben who made me my first club—a driver, of course— and I well remember that he nearly cut his finger off in the process. It was not a great club. An old shaft and an old head were just stuck together in a very rough manner, and the job was finished; but to me that club was one of the most wonderful that had ever been constructed, and at home at nights I studied its many points of excellence until I knew almost every mark that was in the grain of the wood.

The Good Old Days[1]

Suggestions extracted by E. H. Charman

WHILST making no claim to antiquity, the Leicester Golf Club was founded in June 1890 by nine local worthies, most of whose names are still household words in Leicester.

Play was over nine holes on the Leicester Racecourse at Oadby and the course was opened in January 1891, from which it is obvious that not a lot of time was wasted in the preparation of greens and fairways.

In 1892, the membership having increased considerably, the course was transferred to a site on the Stoughton Estate, where it still stands, and the name was changed to Leicestershire Golf Club. At the outset it was graced by a tiny hut which was grandiloquently described as a clubhouse.

What perhaps may be almost unique is the possession by the club of a suggestion book which has been in continuous use since 1894 until 1962 when it became necessary to start a new one.

It is felt that the old book is worthy of a place in the club's archives and it is now kept in the safe—after a narrow escape from destruction by fire.

Much amusement has been derived by members from perusal of this old record of the whims and fancies of our forbears and the writer ventures to think that a few extracts would be of interest to golfers generally.

The first entry, one month after opening the pavilion, seems to indicate early trouble. It reads: 1st November 1894—'The locks require attention as most of the keys supplied are of no use.' The inference is that each member held a key and some were a bit frustrated in their efforts to obtain entry.

The book throughout is full of suggestions for the supply of liquid nourishment of varying brands, tobacco likewise, and food, but I have selected only two extracts which are numbers 2 and 3 in the records.

1. From *Golf Illustrated.*

'3rd November 1894—(a) Suggest that some whisky be kept' and '(b) Also some Guinness.' The Secretary's answer is brief and to the point—'YES.'

Ten days later a fussy member suggests: 'The stove be black-leaded.' One pictures members crowded round a coke stove in the centre of the room.

It does not record whether or not this was done, but, assuming that it was, let us hope that it did not stink too badly!

5th January 1895—'That boxes of fuses may be bought by members.' As it was recorded that this would have attention, let us hope that they were used with care.

5th May 1895—'I strongly object to paying a penny for a score-card.' The secretary was quite pointed about this, saying: 'The ordinary Medal Cards may be had gratis but the council has decided to charge 1*d*. for the Match Cards with Rules, Bogey score etc., which involve considerable cost in printing.' What better evidence of careful stewardship could be desired?

Then come two separate complaints. 1895—(1) 'That two new balls have been stolen from locker 26,' (2) 'Other members have made similar complaints and I suggest a reward of 20*s*. to be offered.' To the first the Secretary replied in effect: 'Keep your locker locked,' and to the second: 'Will ask the Council to give the matter consideration.' Even in these days we can get two new balls for less than £1—and consider the value of the £1 then and nowadays.

14th December 1895—A cry from a frustrated medal winner reads: 'Where are the Medals for Whitsuntide Bank Holiday, 1895?' The reply is twofold: 'The Secretary, who has them, has been ill—on his return they shall be handed over,' then a second thought: 'The Hon. Treasurer now has them; apply to him'—no trouble at all!

4th February 1896—'Having severely torn a golf jacket on the barbed wire at the first hole, I beg to suggest that suitable openings be provided to enable one to get on to the greens in a dignified manner.' The reply is a bit unkind and reads: 'Why not step over it in a dignified manner!'

19th March 1896—'That proper cups be provided for these filthy holes to catch the balls.' Evidently this was not worth an answer, as it has been completely ignored. How primitive could they be. There is evidence that the complaint was still unremedied two or three years later as another member repeats the suggestion.

14th April 1896—Two members sign this one: 'A clean towel or two would be an advantage once a month.' The reply is stern: 'The above remark is evidently intended to be facetious. Clean towels are provided once a week but, as the needs of the Club are growing, it has been arranged that they shall be provided three times a week. Members are reminded that the towels are not intended to clean either clubs or balls as some members seem to think.' A footnote to this reply by the second signatory reads : 'I subscribed to the suggestion in perfect good faith.' Put that in your pipe and smoke it, Mr. Secretary!

15th October 1896—'If two large-sized Clothes Horses were provided, Smith [the professional] could place them round the gas fire and dry wet clothes in the mornings.'

This indicates that the club has progressed in heating arrangements since the days of the coke stove. The suggestion bears a beautiful illustration of an immense clothes horse with garments dangling therefrom and a top hat appearing above the centre, and bare legs at the base! Readers will be pleased to learn that the secretary's answer was; 'Has been attended to.' Let us hope that Smith did not put them too close to the fire. What a job for the 'professional!' How would Henry Cotton have reacted?

8th January 1900—This takes the form of a letter to the secretary and is worth quoting in full :

'Dear Sir, A caddie today insisted on my paying him 1s. for 11 holes, according to the Rules, in spite of the fact that Mr. K.W. had agreed with his caddie that he should carry the two extra holes for 2d. When I was leaving the Club they jeered at me. I spoke to them and warned them but they repeated this conduct. I cannot mention names as the whole lot were implicated but my caddie's name was [sic] Hill. If you could suspend the ringleader I should be grateful. Yours truly, C.S.'

Small wonder the caddie appears to have changed his name! Was his employer's anger really aimed at the boy or was he piqued by the astuteness of his opponent at having made a pre-round bargain at a cut rate! It is interesting that this letter seems to have been a bit too much for the 'powers that were' as no reply was vouchsafed.

June 1901—'Would it not be as well to have the door in the new bicycle house made wide enough to take a tricycle.' Maybe there was more than one 'trike,' as it had attention. It would cause a sensation if any member rolled up on one today!

1907—'That the impediment [a large tree is here depicted] at the last hole be removed—either by dynamite or some more violent explosive.' I bet the complainant had hit the tree a time or two; anyway, he got a reply : 'The suggestion has received the consideration of the Council, but at present it is impossible to get the Estate Authority's consent.' The atomic age had not arrived.

1907—'That a lean-to shed should be erected for motor cars, E.W.K.' A supporter has added: 'Mr. H.C.B. begs to second the proposal. It would be a great help to chauffeurs and a saving to cars which sometimes are obliged to wait in the wet outside.' Nothing doing from the council! Nowadays cars still stand in the wet and there are a heck of a lot of them—without patiently waiting chauffeurs.

17th July 1909—'We suggest that it is desirable whenever there is a sweep that the winner's name be posted up on the notice board— B.A., P.R.W., F.W.F.' This extracted a promise that this should be done and future winners were frustrated from escape from the bar 'incognito.'

15th April 1922—'We have today played cards with a member of the Committee who smoked three "cigars" which he bought from Mrs. Lee. The "cigars" caused considerable comment and annoyance and inquiry elicited the fact that no other brand was kept in the Club. In the interest of Members generally can some decent brand of real cigars be kept; the present ones are unpleasant, and unhealthy, to be in a room with.' Five members signed this—they must have been playing poker. No action is noted but one wag put a pencil note under the suggestion, reading: 'But if he smoked three and survived???'

We now approach more modern days and the suggestions thereafter do not call for comment and, indeed, are best left unnoted, as so many of the signatories are still members of the club. This leads one to reflect that life in the clubhouse and outside is more humdrum than in years gone by—or is it?

The Effect of a Crowd[1]

By Guy B. Farrar

LARGE crowds of spectators at golf matches, perhaps because of their more or less unrestricted movements, can exercise a considerable psychological effect on the result of the play.

This effect may not be in accordance with the wishes of the crowd, they may in fact hinder the triumph of their hero by their intense desire for his success.

The Amateur Championship of 1902, when Harold Hilton and John Lowe were the finalists at St. Andrews, provided an historic instance of the psychological effect a crowd may have on a game.

Hilton, who had been in the lead in the early part of the round, had seen his advantage gradually disappear until the match was all square with two to play. In his *Reminiscences* he gives a dramatic description of how the crowd inadvertently helped him. He writes: 'I was wandering to the 17th tee in a semi-dejected, irritable frame of mind, possibly the worst state a man playing a serious game of golf can drift into, when an excited spectator, caring little and heeding less, made a bee line for a front place, and in his mad career charged full into me. He nearly knocked me over, and as he travelled by on his hurricane passage I could not help hearing the remark: "We'll teach these b——y Englishmen."

'This freely expressed opinion had a most salutary effect upon me: a modified form of anger took the place of the nervous hesitation which pervaded my system, and I said to myself: "Will you?" It was just the necessary antidote I required, and I began to play those last two holes as if they were the only two holes to be played in the championship.'

Hilton played those last two holes so well that he won them both, so the history of the Amateur Championship may well have been changed by the hostile attitude of part of that Scottish crowd, which contributed in no small measure to their hero's defeat.

There have been in the past many occasions when the crowd

1. From *Golf Illustrated*.

through lack of efficient control have made the playing of the game difficult and so had a baleful effect on the golf of a potential champion.

Even when under strict control the tension of playing before a large concourse of ardent admirers and the fear of disappointing their fondest hopes is, I think, a disadvantage which may cause even a seasoned competitor to fail at the critical moment. The urge of the crowd is an undoubted asset in fast-moving team games such as football, but in championship golf there is too much time to weigh up all the dire possibilities, to consider all the disasters that might follow a poor stroke, and the prayerful hopes of a hero-worshipping crowd only add to the almost unsupportable strain of a player with victory in sight.

Few people realize under what nervous strain championship golf is played. A player may seem composed in outward appearance, may play his shots calmly and well, and yet suffer inwardly from acute nervous tension. If you doubt this statement watch his hands. Years ago I remember seeing John Ball playing the 19th hole in a championship match at Hoylake. Outwardly the many times Amateur Champion was complete master of the situation, his face never betraying the slightest sign of emotion, but when he decided to use a new ball his hands were shaking so badly that he had difficulty in removing its paper covering. Incidentally, he hit his drive down the middle of the fairway and won the hole in four.

A well-known Amateur Champion, noted for his calm, majestic appearance on the links, once asked me to lend him a match to light his cigarette whilst he was playing an important and close game in a championship. Nothing could have been more awe-inspiring or stately than this player's outward appearance at that moment, but when he took the match-box in his hand his trembling fingers rattled the matches like castanets. After lighting the cigarette he actually threw my box of matches away and, thanking me, walked on to play his next shot. It was as well that his opponent did not see that incident.

When players are in the state of extreme tension any interference with the run of play, or even any favourable demonstration from the crowd, may break the necessary concentration and cause an unexpected collapse when all seemed set for victory.

The physical advantages of playing before a large crowd are manifest. They act as a wind shield at tees and greens and outline the path to the hole, but their psychological effect may be wholly disastrous, especially to the player who is not accustomed to perform in the limelight of the public's gaze.

All would-be champions, or aspiring internationalists, must overcome the psychological effect that a large crowd may have on their game if they are to reach their ultimate goal.

Length Doesn't Matter[1]

By Dr. Samuel Pope

R EPORTING upon the 1956 Open Golf Championship of Germany at Frankfurt-on-Main, a well-known British golf correspondent wrote: 'The standard of play has been good all through, particularly when one considers that the course is close on 7,000 yards long.' Incidentally, the two players who tied for first place achieved scores of '11 under fours' for the 72 holes.

The lesson to be learned is no new one, namely that length alone fails to provide an adequate test of skill; a test of endurance perhaps, but no golf contest, be it match- or medal-play, was ever intended for that purpose. Nor does the multiplication of penal hazards help to solve the problem.

Twenty-five years ago the Championship Committee were very conscious of the threats which were combining to belittle the problems presented to contestants by our championship courses. The small heavy ball, steel shafts, Gene Sarazen's newly designed sand-iron (precursor of the insidious wedge), and a general improvement in the manicuring of grass were all exerting an influence upon the scoring.

In 1932 the course of the Princes Golf Club at Sandwich was added to the championship rotas as supposedly an answer. From tiger tees it could be stretched to 6,900 yards, and moreover it boasted no fewer than 183 bunkers, mostly designed to punish erring shots.

The result of that championship was a decisive ·defeat of the course by the leading players, so much so that a contemporary critic writing soon afterwards commented that the designers of golf courses had been barking up the wrong tree for the previous 50 years, that additional length was of no avail and that bunkers placed to catch pulled or sliced shots merely served to define the width of fairway, and the more precise judging of distance.

If the good player is to be called upon to produce something more than length and approximate straightness he must be induced to take

1. From *Golf Illustrated*.

risks with his first shot in order to make the next shot easier. Herein lies the golf-course architect's chance. By employing strategically placed bunkers, increased difficulties around the greens (not necessarily sand) in the form of diagonal ridges and hollows—available or added —orientating the greens to receive shots more easily from one or other side of the fairway and not wide open to shots from any angle; the greens themselves not to be excessive in size (650 square yards need seldom be exceeded), nor to be tilted up and well watered to facilitate accurate target practice.

Armed with such terms of reference, the architect has some measure of control against indecent low scoring without recourse to excessive yardage, and skilfully designed holes of under 400 yards in length can provide more exacting 'forms' than holes exceeding 500 yards.

A clear example of this may be seen by examining holes No. 5 and No. 16 on the Old Course at St. Andrews. No. 5, the long hole out, measures 567 yards from the championship tee. There is ample room for a cast drive. The green, probably the largest in the world, can be reached and held from any part of the fairway after a tee shot of adequate length. Such a hole flatters manhood with minimum risk.

No. 16—'corner of the dyke'—which has been stretched for championship purposes to 382 yards, provides the powerful player with a much more difficult task to secure his four. Owing to the centrally placed 'principal's nose' bunker, the direct line and easier approach to the green calls for a drive of courage and accuracy, there being but 30 paces between that bunker and a right-handed 'out of bounds' on to the railway.

The 'safe' line from the tee to the left of the 'principal's nose' brings into play two small bunkers close to the green, and a difficult approach shot to bring off. The green itself presents features so characteristic of St. Andrews, the well-trodden ground rising sharply to its front edge, narrow from front to back, with a tendency to slope away from the player. Suggesting that 'you can't be up without being over', but great is the reward for bravery in the face of danger.

At such a hole the player, whatever his ability, must pay due attention to the dictates of the terrain, which in fact is the principal lesson that St. Andrews offers to those who visit her shrine in search of where her greatness lies. But let the golf-course architect tread warily in his application of this knowledge to restrain big hitters on their native heaths, lest his reputation be cast to perdition, and his pearls to the bulldozer in expiation of his crime of challenging the vanity of tigers.

Moreover, 'added length' will be unneeded for his purpose.

A Good Address

By Bill Cox

MANY mis-hit and mis-timed shots can be attributed to an incorrect address position.

At the address position the left arm, wrist and club should almost be in a straight line and the hands slightly ahead of the club-head.

Most first-class players hold their hands *up* for long shots and *down* for short shots. I often tell my pupils, 'Hands up for power, down for height.'

Let us assume that your grip and stance are correct and the preliminary waggle which precedes the back-swing has been completed; we now come to a very important part of the golf swing—*the forward press*.

Now the forward press varies slightly amongst the leading players. With some it is a distinct sway of the body, with others just a wriggle. In the forward press the club-head should remain stationary behind the ball, whilst the hips move to the left and the hands push the club towards the hole. It is from this position that the back-swing starts.

Many players make the mistake of *leaning* the weight on to the left foot at the address—this causes a steep back-swing and a 'chopping' type of action. The weight should be evenly distributed between the feet; avoid tension, just relax.

Golf with the Red Queen

By Graham Cant

IN COMMON with most other golfers I have often complained of the slowness of other players. And yet I sometimes wonder if a very slow round is any worse than trying to 'save time.' In the one case your concentration doesn't last the full round, in the other you don't concentrate at all!

At one time I used to play quite a lot with an old boy who was absolutely obsessed with time. I used to call him the Red Queen. Remember?

'The Queen said: "Faster! Faster!" and dragged her along. "Are we nearly there?" Alice managed to pant out at last. "Nearly there!" the Queen repeated. "Why, we passed it ten minutes ago! Faster!"'

He was just like that, impelled by some terrible, unreasoning feeling of urgency which allowed no time for the finer points of golfing etiquette, or even a glance at the scenery that flashed by. I don't think it was a form of gamesmanship. Like Captain Hook's crocodile, he must have swallowed a clock at some time.

He would open his campaign on the first tee. 'We're going to be held up!' he would cry. As, at his special request, we invariably played at a time when normal players were eating their lunches, this would come as a bit of a surprise. A careful scrutiny of the terrain, however, might reveal a solitary pair of figures putting out on the distant 5th green. Unmindful of their coming doom, the little victims played.

The Red Queen would then seize the honour and having driven off—this was in the days before caddie carts were invented—he would grab both bags of clubs and stand poised on one foot, rather like an elderly model for the statue of Eros in Piccadilly Circus. The start of my back-swing would be the signal to go, and with his flying start he used to make quite a good race of it with my ball. Admittedly, this didn't call for any great turn of speed, but how he avoided being decapitated by the slice I could never make out. He always stood by

---

1. From *Golf Illustrated*.

the tee-box. A break on the blind side would not have been nearly as effective.

This would go on all round the course, finishing on the last green by his looking at the clock and muttering: 'Two hours and ten minutes! I haven't enjoyed that!' Needless to say, he wore out partners at a prodigious rate, but I was quite interested in trying to think out counter-moves, such as stopping to light a cigarette on each tee in the hope that the weight of both bags might tire him out. It never did, and the habit became prohibitively expensive. To simply outrun him would have been unfair, for he was a great deal older than I was.

It was interesting, too, to see how he dealt with that slow pair we last saw holing out at the 5th. When we eventually overtook them, and we always did, he would putt out at a gallop, rush over to the next tee and stand rigidly to attention with a look of concentrated hatred on his face. Few players could stand it for more than a couple of holes before their nerve broke. He was seldom reduced to the necessity of actually having to ask to go through.

The Red Queen was not unique in his efforts to speed up the game, nor am I the only partner to have suffered similar attentions. Modern golf is certainly too slow, but, as we say in Fife, there's a mids in a'thing, and that's no' it.

Thumbs Down the Shaft[1]

By Tom Vardon

MONEY was much scarcer in Jersey than in other places, and there was little or none of it for the boys, so that there were no drivers for them and no golf clubs properly made at all. What we did in these circumstances was to get a head of any kind from somewhere, perhaps one that had been broken off from another club and discarded, and an odd shaft that had been abandoned in the same way, and these we pieced together in the best way we could. They made very inefficient weapons, but they were the best we could lay hands on, and even they were a great advance on the primitive affairs that we originally made for ourselves from the branches that we cut in the woods.

By the way, when I mention the branches I should like to call attention to a little peculiarity in the game of both Harry and myself, for which these tree clubs were entirely responsible in the first place. For a long time we were almost alone in first-class golf as players who put their thumbs down the shafts of their wooden clubs when playing with them, and the habit was generally condemned as being bad and interfering with the drive, though during the last few years this opinion has been very much revised, and one now sees an increasing number of golfers gripping their clubs with the left thumb down the shaft. I am a very firm believer in gripping in this way, and I know that Harry is also, for we hold that the club is steadied and guided in this way as it could be in no other. Nevertheless, we did not come to grip in this way because we had thought the question out on these lines, but in a quite accidental manner. When we played as small boys with our roughly cut blackthorn shafts we were unable to place any covering on the handles, and to make matters worse these were generally fairly well covered with knots in the wood, which we trimmed and smoothed down as much as possible, but which still were hard and rough to the hand. We found that when we grasped these handles with the thumbs round the shafts they bruised our hands very much,

1. From *Great Golfers in the Making* (Methuen).

Golfers' hazard. English golfers, to whom immaculate greens are merely commonplace, will be interested in this picture, from the Griquatown Golf Course, Griqualand West, South Africa. When players reach the 'green' there they find putting impossible because of the thick sand, so they are allowed to place their ball on a hardened strip at a distance from the cup equal to that at which it finished up on the approach shot

The 48-tee double-decker driving range at Finchley

made them too sore for us to play, and at times even cut us, and we found that the best and only certain cure for the trouble, short of putting on proper grips, which seemed out of the question, was to grip with our thumbs down the shaft, and so we did accordingly.

We grew up to the habit, and have experienced no desire to desert it, notwithstanding that the majority of our contemporaries favoured another kind of grip and have challenged the efficiency of ours; and now, as I have said, I believe that ours has merits that are possessed by no other. What an insignificant little thing in golf must seem to the outsider this question of whether a man shall place his thumb along the shaft or at the side of it; but the old player knows of what mighty importance are these small details!

Planning the Hazards[1]

By W. Herbert Fowler

IN AUGUST 1902 I began to survey Walton Heath with a view to making an 18-hole course on it for Mr. Cosmo Bonsor and others. The heath was at that time entirely covered with heather from two feet to three feet deep, and it was somewhat difficult to know where to go; but by the aid of much riding and walking I finally came to the conclusion that in a certain spot I could make two extra good short holes, and I worked backwards and forwards from the present 6th[2] hole (happily named by Mr. Justice Bucknill 'Port Arthur'), and after much thought and some changes the present course was laid out.

The placing of the bunkers has caused much discussion, but the main theory on which I worked was that most bad shots are either slices or pulls, and that all hazards across a course are liable to become unfair when a strong wind blows, whereas side hazards are never so affected. I believe that as time goes on we shall find that this theory will gain ground, and it must always be remembered that it is far easier to carry a hazard than to avoid one.

Another strong reason in favour of side hazards seems to me to be that the weaker drivers are not too severely penalized for their want of power. I think there can be no doubt that the player who plays most of his golf on such a course will find the cross hazard or 'steeple-chase' course very easy by comparison and not half so interesting to play on.

---

1. From *Great Golfers in the Making* (Methuen).
2. Now the 7th.

Early Days[1]

By Willie Auchterlonie

(Open Champion, 1893)

WE WERE not nearly so particular in the matter of clubs in those days—naturally, from the force of circumstances—as we are now, and I can very well remember the sort of things that had to do duty for them at that time. For wooden clubs any kind of old head and old shaft we could come across was made to serve our purpose, and if they happened, by good luck, to be joined together as a complete club when they came into our possession, then so much the better. But if we chanced to get them separately, then we proceeded to fasten them together by melting down a piece of an old gutta-percha ball, and most religiously would we save up any little fragments of old broken gutta balls that we had for this purpose, and this we would use instead of glue, and it seemed to do very well, too, as a substitute. We afterwards put on string or proper tarry 'waupin', if we were fortunate enough to have a piece of it, in as good an imitation of the orthodox manner as we could.

As for iron clubs of any kind, they were very difficult indeed for us to get at that time, and practically the only way in which we could ever manage to get possession of one was by going, two or three of us together, to old Bob Wilson's smith, which stood a little way along North Street from where I have said we used to play at the lampposts, and there lend him a hand by working round his turning lathe for him, because, as he did not have steam power for this purpose, it all had to be done by the hand; and then occasionally for our services in this way we would get some old or spoiled head from him, and very proud indeed we were whenever this happened.

Of course, I need scarcely say who this old Bob Wilson was, as almost every golfer knows or has heard of him. He was the first man to make iron club-heads here in St. Andrews, and these heads of his make are valuable yet, both for playing with and as curiosities, especially those with the famous horse-shoe nail in them at the back of the blade.

1. From *Great Golfers in the Making* (Methuen).

The Day a Man went Mad

By Tony Strange

BRITAIN, sad to say, is badly off for world records in sport. Think for a moment or two. How many current world-record holders can you recall? There are precious few.

Take golf. The United Strates with Arnold Palmer and Jack Nicklaus have a formidable pair who are almost unbeatable by the rest of the world except when, from time to time, men like Gary Player snatch away a dollar or two.

Indeed, these are the players who have taken over from golf's previous rulers, the Cottons, Hogans, Lockes and Sneads. But surprise —despite this illustrious array of golfing power, past and present, a British player from Scotland, Tom Haliburton, still holds the world record for the lowest two consecutive rounds of tournament golf.

It is a record which has stood the test of time, for only Snead has equalled it since Haliburton, the Ryder Cup player, produced a 61 and then a 65 for an aggregate of 126 in the opening two rounds of the Spalding tournament at Worthing, Sussex, on 12th and 13th June 1952.

Consider the number of tournaments which have been played since that time throughout the world and think of the great players who have competed in them. Weigh up these two factors and the magnitude of Haliburton's achievement, which upset the previous best by Hogan two years earlier at White Sulphur Springs, Virginia, by two shots, will be more than appreciated.

With all Britain's professionals and a sprinkling of overseas competitors assembled at the Sussex seaside resort for yet another 72-hole stroke-play event, which at that time over-burdened the calendar, Haliburton was hardly the form selection.

The Scot was one of the more consistent rather than spectacular golfers in the field and if at that time anyone had been asked what they thought of his chances, the answer would have been, 'Tom will finish with the leaders or thereabouts.'

That was before Haliburton's golfing dream came true and lasted two whole days. It was rather like getting the Treble Chance football pool correct to win a cool million. During that time he played every shot and putt with super-human control. He was a man inspired.

Iron play was deadly accurate and the rare mistake was quickly smoothed away with a delicate chip or a bold putt. Naturally, in a game where a wormcast can deflect a drive into cruel rough, Haliburton enjoyed just that element of good fortune which always settles on men who conquer the world. In this respect the Scot took inspiration from the two chip shots he holed for birdie threes at the 2nd and 5th holes.

On this rolling course laced attractively across the Downs with all its greens—or so they say—running towards the sea, his scoring was unbelievable. He reached the turn in 29 with an impressive line-up of birdies—432, 434, 333.

The modest Haliburton was surely wondering how long these kind of crazy figures would go on stringing themselves together. But they did and his homeward trip looked just as crazy—334, 434, 443—and he was back in the clubhouse with a 61.

Haliburton, happy as a man who had taken a dram too many, spoke the truth when he declared in the changing-room, 'I can't believe it.'

At that point in the proceedings he had equalled the lowest British tournament round. But what was to happen the next day to the man who was said to lack golfing stamina? In golf, anticlimax very often partners success. But on this occasion the bar critics were wrong.

The following day Haliburton was in the same devastating mood and he went out to produce a 65 for the world record. It was incredible. It was golf the easy way, especially when he holed a full No. 5 iron shot to the 15th hole for an albatross 2. That was his moment of genius.

The final two rounds were a disappointment. What should have been victory in a canter for Haliburton was instead inglorious defeat. The Scot went out in the third round with a seven-shot lead over the field, and it seemed that, even if he could not maintain the phenomenal brand of golf, the £300 first prize was his beyond dispute.

Perhaps the sparkling performance dazzled and dazed him. Maybe he had his eye on yet another world record. With his halfway total of 126 on the board, Haliburton needed to add another 132 shots over 36 holes to dispossess Hogan and joint holder Byron Nelson of the 72-hole record which stood at 259.

Who knows what agonies Haliburton endured in that flush of success. The tension as he waited to drive off under the gaze of a massed gallery must have been electric inside him—butterflies jet-propelled.

Everybody was thinking of records but the outlook was not encouraging. A sea mist lay ominously over the Downs blotting out the 6,376-yard course and even an inspired golfer with a magic touch needed reasonable visibility to see which way he should go.

For six holes it was a game of blind man's bluff and not a very enjoyable one either. Poor Haliburton! His shots no longer came off. He missed greens. Putts were off target. He had lost his touch.

By the time the fog lifted and he emerged into the clear, the Scot's game was shattered. It was generally felt by those who sadly watched the collapse that the experience over the two previous days had completely unnerved him. He finished the terrifying round in 75 and with a 72 in the afternoon Haliburton's dreams had dissolved into thin air. His lead had gone and his final total of 273 forced him back into fourth place behind Harry Weetman, Antonio Cerda and Bill Shankland.

Haliburton had no excuses. He did not blame the fog but instead frankly admitted, 'I could not keep it up and that's all there is to it.'

That's typical of Tom Haliburton. He's a fine sportsman and the kind of man who should rightly hold world records.

Although most golfers have forgotten this tremendous feat members of the Worthing club are for ever reminded of Haliburton's achievement.

It is recorded for posterity on a stone bench beside the first tee—cold comfort for those waiting their turn to drive off!

Hit and Miss[1]

By John L. Low

IN THE field political I look back with greatest pleasure on the effort I made with Mr. Mure Ferguson and the leading professionals to stop the use of the easily driven patent balls which were introduced in 1902. Today I do not suppose that there is a single golfer of note, with the possible exception of Mr. Hutchinson, who does not regret that our policy failed to find proper support at the time. Every shade and grade of indifferent golfer saw that at length his chance had come of beating the men whose skill had long defied him. Players who had practically never been beaten by the second- and third-class men now found themselves liable to defeat in any chance round. Apart altogether from the fact that the holes became automatically shorter, the less skilful player became a force to be dreaded for two reasons, which have been so well stated by two great players that quotation only is necessary. Harry Vardon, in an oft-quoted sentence, pointed out that the soft ball gave the player his *'two chances*, the hit *and* the miss.' And Mr. John Ball, in an even more subtly piercing dictum, pointed out that the rubber-cored ball *does away with the bad lie,* and consequently with the skill formerly required in making long shots from unfavourable positions with wooden clubs. Every influence was brought to bear against us, and the selfishness of the arguments used by some of our opponents passes the power of expression to denounce. That these men found their fool's paradise disappear, when at the end of a six months' trial the links were lengthened, is a matter of some satisfaction : but that the game should have lost much of its past athletic quality must always be a thing much to be regretted. Looking backward, then, I find my greatest satisfaction in the thought that I was associated with those who in that crisis worked for the honour of the great game.

1. From *Great Golfers in the Making* (Methuen).

Coaxing Back the Skill[1]

By James Braid

ONE'S experience as a golfer seems to be all morals and nothing else but morals. One hardly ever goes out for a round, even in these days of championship, without having some cold truth, which had been temporarily neglected, thrust home to one's mind with nerve-straining force, as if the gods of golf were angered because their laws should be treated so carelessly. There is so much to remember in this game, and when one has been playing well for a little time it is so easy to become over-confident, and exist in the belief that you can do the shots anyhow and cannot miss them. For a day it may seem so, and then, alas! that fine game has gone away for a long season, and that foolish golfer who cherished it too little is left lamenting and foozling. Here, indeed, while one is only wondering what to say upon the subject, is a moral, and as it seems to me a big one, provided automatically—that it is never more necessary to be careful and thoughtful than when one is playing well; never more necessary to husband carefully every detail of the skill that one has acquired, and study it down to the pressure of the little finger, lest perchance when the skill goes away for a time—as it does with all of us now and then—one may be left without the secrets of coaxing it back again.

---

1. From *Great Golfers in the Making* (Methuen).

The Freemasonry of Golf

By Webster Evans

NO GAME, I suppose, has ever had such an amazing rise in popularity as golf has had since 1890. These last 70-odd years have
seen it grow from a game played by few and watched by practically
nobody to a game played and watched by millions all over the world.

The attitude of the man-in-the-street towards the game changed
completely and nowhere is this more clearly seen than in the pages
of *Punch*. In the early 'nineties Mr. Punch's artists saw golfers as
eccentrics—amiable and (fairly) harmless maybe, but eccentrics all
the same. 'Mummy,' says a little boy as he sees a knickerbockered
figure carrying a bag of golf clubs over his shoulder, 'Mummy, what's
that man *for?*' Golfers, in the drawings of Raven Hill, George du
Maurier, Phil May and the rest were always irascible colonels or irate
admirals or, as a change, anaemic-looking curates or mannish women.

Then suddenly *Punch* seemed to realize that golf had 'arrived'
and there appeared a brilliant cartoon entitled 'The Golf Stream',
in which men of all ages and women and children, too, are seen
streaming along with clubs in their hands or slung over their shoulders.
Golf was no longer just a joke.

Why did golf have this amazing growth from 1890 onwards?
The main reason, of course, was that the English middle classes suddenly took it up in a big way and their lead was followed in the United
States, on the Continent and throughout the Empire. In 1890 there
were only some 50 clubs in England, fewer than 20 in the United
States and only a handful elsewhere. The only tournaments as such
were the Open and Amateur Championships and these were hardly
noticed in the Press, although there had been a number of books on
the game.

As the 'nineties moved on, however, the golf bomb burst. The
newspapers began to give more space to it, particularly when a leading
politician, Arthur Balfour, later to be Prime Minister, showed almost as
must interest in the game as General Eisenhower does today. Golf
began to have official blessing; if Mr. Balfour played it and wrote

'D'you mind drinking out of the bottle, sir?
We seem to have run out of glasses.'

about it and urged other people to buy it, well, it couldn't be just a pastime for eccentrics. In later years other men in the public eye—notably Mr. Lloyd George and the Prince of Wales (remember his Fair-Isle sweaters?)—led the golf fashion, as it were.

Before the 'nineties very few people had ever heard of any of the leading players; they might recognize the bearded face of Old Tom Morris, but nobody else. Then suddenly the names of Harry Vardon, J. H. Taylor, James Braid, John Ball, Harold Hilton and Freddy Tait began to appear in the newspapers. And when the gallant Tait, an officer in the Black Watch, was killed in the Boer War, even non-golfers read about it with regret. Golf had become news; and nobody saw this more clearly than the brilliant young newspaper proprietor Alfred Harmsworth, later Lord Northcliffe. Golf was given plenty of space in the pages of his up-and-coming newspaper, the *Daily Mail*. Other papers, too, began to report golf and there arose a new class of sports writer, the golf journalist, men like Henry Leach, Horace Hutchinson, Bernard Darwin and their successors.

And soon they began to have the great visiting Americans to write about, for golf had spread like a prairie fire across the States. Walter Hagen and Bobby Jones, in particular, brought glamour and colour to the game—Hagen for his mannerisms and smart clothes and easy air of opulent confidence, Jones for the superb artistry of his golf. And our own stars—particularly Henry Cotton, the first of what may be called the Public School type of professional—became household names, even to non-golfers, through the newspapers. And, as time went on, there were the three leading Anglo-American contests to write about—the Walker, Ryder and Curtis Cups.

But I am getting ahead of myself. Apart from the general spread of the game and the consequent publicity, what other factors were there that gave an added fillip to the game? There were three chief factors, I think, and some subsidiary ones. The three chief factors were the coming of the rubber-cored ball that made the game easier to play; the coming of the internal combustion engine that enabled people to travel more easily to the golf course; and the fact that women found that golf was a game that suited them admirably.

Up to 1902 golf was played with the gutta-percha ball—the old 'guttie'. Although Freddy Tait had driven a 'guttie' 280 yards, all carry, and other 'tigers' did marvellous things with it, the 'rabbit' found it hard to get up into the air; golf for him was a toilsome and unrewarding pursuit. The coming of the rubber-cored ball—invented at the turn of the century by an American named Coburn Haskell— made golf a much easier and more pleasant game for the *average* golfer to play. He could have a not-very-good shot and get away with it in a manner quite impossible with a 'guttie'.

As balls improved, so did transport. Before the coming of the motor car the golfer had to get to the club on his feet, on a bicycle, in a horse-drawn vehicle of some sort or by train. In the early days of the twentieth century all the main lines ran special trains for London golfers and many provincial golfers had similar facilities. But can you imagine your golf club without a car-park and without a single car? Once one could just jump into a car and drive up to the club, golf became a game for Mr. and Mrs. Everyman and their family.

For the cars brought the ladies to the club as well as the men. In 1890 there was no Ladies Championship and indeed golfing ladies were treated as even more of a joke by cartoonists—and by the world in general—than the men were. It was thought unladylike even to want to hit the ball more than about 50 yards. But, in spite of ridicule, the pioneer ladies persevered and in 1893 the first Ladies Championship was held and won by the almost legendary Lady Margaret Scott, whose retirement after winning the title three times running was as graceful as her flowing swing must have been. Some years, of course, were to elapse before ladies' golf really became news—until the days, in fact, when Miss Cecil Leitch and Miss Joyce Wethered brought skill and strength as well as grace to the links.

The golf ball, as I have said, was revolutionized by Haskell's invention; it might also be said that the golf club was revolutionized by the invention of the stainless-steel head and the tubular steel shaft. Stainless steel cut out all the sand-papering once needed to keep the heads clean and rust-proof; but this was not nearly such a revolution as the steel shaft. There had been a patent for a type of steel shaft way back in the 'nineties, but it was a clumsy affair and never caught on. Hickory was what you made shafts out of—and a wonderful feel a fine hickory-shafted club had, too. Yet there is no doubt that the steel shaft—not legalized until 1929—made golf an easier, and therefore more popular, game to play.

All golf equipment has improved, adding to the popularity of the game. Peg tees, of wood or plastic, are much handier than the pinch of sand one used to extract from the sand-box on the teeing ground; waterproof clothing of all kinds has made wet-weather golf more endurable; the modern hooded bag, with its capacious pockets for carrying practically everything except the kitchen sink, is better than the old drainpipe affair of the past—even if it does need a trolley to carry it. The mechanical caddie has superseded for most of us the human bag-carrier of previous days, with his faults and virtues. Did you know, by the way, that *Punch* in the early years of this century had a cartoon entitled 'Mr. Punch's Patent Caddie Car', showing a boy pushing a little cart containing not only a bag of clubs but a decanter of whisky, a syphon of soda-water and two glasses? There is indeed nothing new under the sun!

Not only did equipment improve, but courses became better kept, too, as the years went by. Modern machinery made upkeep easier, greens became smoother and the rough on the whole much less fierce; all things that, accumulatively, helped towards the growth of golf. Golf in 1890 was a game played by only a few thousand people; now it is played and enjoyed by millions all over the world. Then it was a free-and-easy game played by a few devotees, mainly in Scotland; now it is a world-wide sporting organization.

I would like to end by quoting some words of wisdom written by one of the earliest of golf writers, Henry Leach. 'Golf', he said, 'may be, and is, used by people of every colour, race, creed and temperament, in every climate and all the year round. No recreation, apart from the simplest contests of the river and field, has been so universal since the world began, with the single exception of chess. There is no freemasonry like the freemasonry of golf.' And so say all of us.

Remove some of those Bunkers[1]

By Guy B. Farrar

'WHEN she calls lavender, summer must die.' As the London lavender-sellers of long ago in Patrick Chalmer's poem foretold the death of summer, so the coming of autumn each year heralds the end of another season of competitive golf.

Autumn, a time for reconstruction and repair, a time when green committees consider alterations which may modernize their course or add a 'new look' to some hole that has slowly deteriorated with the silent alchemy of the passing years.

With the present cost of labour and materials, major alterations might be ruled out on the score of expense, but sometimes considerable improvements can be effected at little cost, by merely altering the line of play at a hole and at the same time bringing into play some natural feature such as a grassy hollow or sandhill, an area of gorse or rushes, or, on inland courses, a clump of trees or bushes.

In spite of the old joke, obviously untrue, about a club who wrote to the Royal and Ancient Golf Club concerning some point of the rules in relation to trees and received the reply 'There are no trees on St. Andrews' links', I do not see any objection to trees being used as hazards provided that an all-seeing Providence has planted them in a suitable position.

I know of two isolated trees in the centre of a fairway which provide alternative lines of approach to the green in the same manner as the Principal's Nose, the famous St. Andrews' bunker at the 16th hole.

If an alternative approach can be arranged by means of a hazard in the centre of the fairway, and the more courageous tee shot reaps the reward of an easier second, then that hole will present a tactical problem from the tee and any hole that needs consideration before playing it must be interesting.

An altered tee giving a new line of play can often transform a dull,

1. From *Golf Illustrated.*

straight hole into a testing dog-leg, though such an alteration might also call for some slight rearrangement of the bunkering guarding the green.

Even without altering the position of the tee a straight hole can be made to play like a dog-leg by making it slightly easier, and therefore more desirable, to play the approach from one side of the fairway rather than from the centre. The key bunker, or other hazard, is the one that decides which is the easiest line of approach and consequently the best line for the tee shot. This line should not necessarily be the obvious one, the thinking golfer will soon discover it for himself.

Improvements and economies can often be effected by filling up redundant bunkers or converting them into grass hollows. The difficulty is to convince members that a bunker is unnecessary, especially if one of their recent opponents has been unlucky enough to be trapped by it. The old idea that a bunker's chief function was to penalize a bad shot dies hard.

The filling up of useless bunkers will certainly make any course harder for a good player because he has been deprived of his ancient landmarks on which he often based his judgement of the length of shot and so the selection of the appropriate club.

The old-fashioned cross-bunker, so beloved of a past generation of green committees, is a typical example of a helpful hazard. A good player knew that if he pitched over the cross-bunker his ball was certain to be hole high. Take away the cross-bunker and there is no aid to judging distance except the appearance of the flagstick or possibly the edge of the green, usually a very indistinct aiming mark.

Many years ago I played a round on a newly constructed course before any hazards were made. Judging distance was then a major problem. I have played the same course many times since the bunkering was completed, but never found it so difficult as on that original visit.

Discussing the prospects of a rising young professional with a well-known golfing critic some years ago, we agreed that he had all the shots plus a good golfing temperament, but the critic added : 'He will never reach the top, he is such a poor judge of distance.'

The importance of judging distance is second only to the importance of style and temperament, so that any removal of aids to judging distance must add to the playing difficulties of a course.

Consider each bunker in its relation to the play of the hole and if you can honestly say that it has no effect on the line of play and is merely there to punish any shot unlucky enough to reach it, then it is redundant and its removal will improve that hole.

There are hundreds of unnecessary bunkers on courses in Britain. They cost clubs pounds to maintain the sand—an expensive item on inland courses these days. As well there is the constant attention they require from green-keepers, who could be more usefully employed on other more deserving parts of the course.

Our Happy Game
By Henry Leach

GOLF may be, and is, used by people of every colour, race, creed and temperament, in every climate and all the year round. No recreation, apart from the simplest contests of the river and field, has been so universal since the world began, with the single exception of chess. And wherever and whenever it is played it extends its benign influence towards the promotion of fast friendship among the players. There is no freemasonry like the freemasonry of golf. To its temples in every land are always welcomed the faithful and earnest craftsman from where'er he came, and he is passed on the signs of the bag and the stance and the little pimpled ball. For it is one of the articles of belief that no man can be a good and enthusiastic golfer of experience and at the same time a thoroughly bad fellow, for at the outset of his career the bad fellow would never be happy in his game. . . . Thus has our happy game of golf wound a bright cordon round the world, and so does she play her part in the great evolution of general contentment.